The
Maryland Colony

by Dennis Brindell Fradin

CHILDREN'S PRESS
A Division of Grolier Publishing
Sherman Turnpike
Danbury, Connecticut 06816

For their help, the author thanks the staff of the
Maryland Historical Society in Baltimore, Maryland.

Library of Congress Cataloging-in-Publication Data

Fradin, Dennis B.
    The Maryland Colony / by Dennis B. Fradin.
        p. cm.
    At head of title: The thirteen colonies.
    Includes index.
    Summary: Examines the history of Maryland, from its colonization by
England to the early years of its statehood. Includes brief biographical
sketches of key figures.
    ISBN 0-516-00394-1
    1. Maryland—History—Colonial period, ca. 1600-1775—Juvenile literature.
2. Maryland—History—Colonial period, ca. 1600-1775—Biography—Juvenile
literature. 3. Maryland—History—Revolution, 1775-1783—Juvenile literature.
4. Maryland—History—Revolution, 1775-1783—Biography—Juvenile
literature. [1. Maryland—History—Colonial period, ca. 1600-1775.
2. Maryland—History—Revolution, 1775-1783.] I. Title. II. Title: Thirteen
colonies.
F184.F73   1990
975.2'02—dc20   90-2210
                                                                   CIP
                                                                    AC

5 6 7 8 9 10 R 99 98 97 96 95

Table of Contents

Maryland's forests (left) provided game and timber for the early settlers. Chesapeake Bay (below), which teemed with fish and shellfish, was a rich fishing ground, as it is today.

Chapter I

Introducing the Old Line State

This [the Potomac River] is the sweetest and greatest river I have ever seen. . . . The soil [in the Maryland region] is so excellent that we cannot set down a foot, but tread on strawberries, raspberries, fallen mulberry vines, acorns, walnuts, sassafras. . . . All is high woods except where the Indians have cleared for corn. It abounds with delicate springs which are our best drinks. Birds diversely feathered there are infinite, as eagles, swans, herons, geese, bitterns, ducks, partridge . . . and the like, by which will appear, the place abounds not alone with profit, but also with pleasure.

From Relation of Maryland *(1635), by Father Andrew White, one of the first Maryland colonists*

Maryland is a small state on the east coast of the United States. It was one of the thirteen American colonies that England founded or conquered along the east coast in the 1600s and 1700s. The other twelve colonies were New Hampshire, Massachusetts, Rhode Island, Connecticut, New York, Pennsylvania, New Jersey, Delaware, Virginia, North Carolina, South Carolina, and Georgia.

Maryland is shaped somewhat like a squirt gun. Chesapeake Bay, an arm of the Atlantic Ocean, divides Maryland into two parts, called the Eastern Shore and the Western Shore. Pennsylvania is Maryland's neighboring state to the north. Delaware and the Atlantic Ocean form Maryland's eastern border. Virginia, West Virginia, and Washington, D.C. (the nation's capital) are Maryland's neighbors to the south and the west.

Even though Maryland is closer to Maine than it is to Florida, Maryland is often called a Southern state. One reason for this is that for most of colonial times, Maryland was in the southern half of the English colonies. Florida belonged to Spain, while Georgia wasn't settled by England until 1733. Also, tobacco growing and slavery, which were more associated with the South than with the North, were important in early Maryland.

However, Maryland also has much in common with the Northern states. During the Civil War (1861–1865), which the Northern and Southern states fought over slavery and other issues, Maryland sided with the North. Maryland's largest city, Baltimore, resembles other Northern cities in many ways. All things considered, it is probably best to think of Maryland as a gateway between the North and South.

Many important historical events have taken place in Maryland. The Maryland Colony was founded in the 1630s by George and Cecil Calvert, a father and son who were the first two Lords Baltimore. The Calverts made Maryland a place where Roman Catholics and other persecuted people could live in peace. The city of Baltimore, the songbirds known as Baltimore orioles, and the Baltimore Orioles baseball team were all named for the Lords Baltimore.

George Calvert

The Calverts controlled Maryland for most of its more than 140 years as an English colony. Then from 1775 to 1783 the thirteen colonies fought the Revolutionary War to break free of Great Britain. George Washington, the American commander, praised Maryland's "troops of the line" for the bravery of these soldiers in fighting the British. Because of this, Maryland is nicknamed the *Old Line State.*

Cecil Calvert

During the United States early years, the national capital moved from city to city. Two Maryland cities—Baltimore and Annapolis—briefly served as the U.S. capital between 1776 and 1784. Washington, D.C., which became the

7

Meeting place of Congress in Baltimore in 1776

Francis Scott Key

permanent U.S. capital in the year 1800, was carved out of a piece of Maryland.

Just a few years after Maryland gave up the land for Washington, D.C., the national anthem was written in the state. The year was 1814, and the United States was again fighting the British in what was called the War of 1812. In September 1814, British ships fired on Fort McHenry, which guarded Baltimore. They hoped to take the fort and burn Baltimore. A Marylander named Francis Scott Key watched the bombardment from a nearby boat but could not see who had won the battle because the smoke was so thick. Then, by the dawn's early light, Key saw that the United States flag was still flying over Fort McHenry. The

British had not taken the fort and would not seize Baltimore. This inspired Key to write "The Star-Spangled Banner."

Nearly 50 years later, in 1862, an event with a much sadder outcome took place in Maryland. On September 17, 1862, during the Civil War, the Battle of Antietam was fought near Hagerstown. About 24,000 soldiers were killed or wounded in this Northern victory, making it the bloodiest one-day battle of the Civil War.

One big change that has taken place in Maryland during the 1800s and 1900s concerns the

Antietam National Battlefield near Sharpsburg, Maryland, commemorates the Battle of Antietam.

way its people earn their living. Nearly everyone in colonial America farmed and only a small percentage of people worked in industry. Today this situation is reversed in Maryland and most other states. Packaged foods, metals, and electrical equipment are among Maryland's main products. Baltimore is the state's manufacturing center as well as one of the major port cities in the country. About half of all Marylanders live in—or close to—Baltimore. Because of the government offices in the Washington, D.C. region, many Marylanders work for the government.

The modern skyline of Baltimore

Considering its size (only eight states are smaller), Maryland has been the home of a remarkable number of famous people. Benjamin Banneker (1731–1806), a black scientist who helped lay out the boundaries of Washington, D.C., was born near Baltimore. Elizabeth Ann Seton (1774–1821) was born in New York City but lived for more than ten years in Maryland. She started the first Catholic elementary school in the United States in Baltimore. In 1975, Elizabeth Ann Seton became the first person born in the United States to be declared a saint by the Roman Catholic Church.

Roger Taney (1777–1864), who was born in Calvert County, served as attorney general under President Andrew Jackson and later was the fifth chief justice of the Supreme Court of the United States. Frederick Douglass (1818?–1895) and Harriet Tubman (1820?–1913) began life as slaves on Maryland's Eastern Shore. Douglass, who was born near Easton, wrote a famous autobiography called *Narrative of the Life of Frederick Douglass* and also founded an antislavery newspaper called the *North Star*. Harriet Tubman, who was born near Cambridge, was the most famous "conductor" on the Underground Railroad, the system that helped slaves escape northward to freedom.

Benjamin Banneker

Roger Taney

Harriet Tubman

Frederick Douglass

Francis Scott Key (1779-1843), of "Star-Spangled Banner" fame, was born in what is now Carroll County. Edgar Allan Poe (1809-1849), the author of such famous horror stories as "The Tell-Tale Heart" and "The Black Cat," was born in Boston, Massachusetts, but at the age of 20 he moved to Baltimore where he lived for a few years. George Herman "Babe" Ruth (1895-1948), the great baseball player who belted 714 home runs in his major-league career, was born in Baltimore.

Besides its fascinating history and many famous people, Maryland has many natural treasures. One of the most precious of these is Chesapeake Bay, which is used for swimming, boating, and fishing. Thanks in large part to Chesapeake Bay, Maryland is one of the leading states in the production of oysters, soft-shell clams, and crabs. Of the many lovely rivers that flow through Maryland, the Potomac is the best known. The Potomac, which forms Maryland's border with Virginia and most of its border with West Virginia, is the river on which Washington, D.C., is located. Other important Maryland rivers include the Susquehanna, Pocomoke, Wicomico, Nanticoke, Choptank, Elk, Patuxent, Patapsco, and Severn. The western part of Maryland contains the lovely Blue Ridge and Allegheny

Left: Chesapeake Bay is famous for its oyster fisheries.
Below: The wild ponies of Assateague Island

Mountains. Maryland's highest peak, Backbone Mountain, rises to a height of 3,360 feet in the Allegheny Mountains.

The mountains, woods, and wetlands of Maryland contain a great deal of wildlife, although not as much as when Indians were the only people who lived there. Deer, foxes, and bears are still found in the state, as are many kinds of ducks and other waterfowl. Assateague Island, which lies off Maryland's shore, is famous for its wild ponies. And Baltimore orioles—the state bird—can still be seen flying in the Old Line State.

SASQUESAHANOK

A Susquehannock Indian village

Chapter II

The Indians of Maryland

The Indians were largely peaceful. The Maryland leaders made a conscious effort to avoid conflicts with the local Indians that might lead to warfare. . . . The natives responded with a willingness to teach the English how to make corn bread and hominy, to show them what herbs and roots could be used for medicines and dyes, to make them log canoes, and to help in other ways. If the Indians had decided on war, the infant colony might not have survived. As it was, while relationships were often uneasy, no major hostilities broke out.

From an essay by Russell Menard and Lois Carr in the book Early Maryland in a Wider World

People first arrived in Maryland at least 10,000 years ago. The first Marylanders were Indians who hunted with stone-tipped spears and made bowls and pottery. The tools made by these prehistoric Marylanders have been unearthed.

The Indian tribes that lived in Maryland in more recent times may have been related to the ancient Indians. Among the tribes of the Eastern Shore were the Nanticokes, Choptanks, Pocomokes, and Wicomicos. On the Western Shore lived the Piscataway and Patuxent tribes. All these tribes have rivers named for them. At Chesapeake Bay's northern end near the Susquehanna River lived the Susquehannock tribe.

Maryland's Indians lived in villages, some of which were surrounded by wooden fences called palisades. Several hundred people lived in the smaller villages. One Susquehannock village near the Maryland-Pennsylvania border had several thousand people in the mid-1600s.

The Indians built the frames for their *wigwams* (homes) out of wood, and covered them with tree bark. A typical wigwam housed about ten people, most of them related. Although some men had more than one wife, a family usually consisted of two parents, their children, and a few other relatives.

The family slept on wooden platforms that were covered by furs and mats. They used the area beneath the platforms to store such household items as bowls and tools. They sat on mats to eat their meals. The families ate from wooden bowls and used shells as spoons. Food was cooked over an indoor fire. A hole in the roof allowed the smoke to escape.

Men's work included hunting, fishing, and building canoes and weapons. The men used

This drawing shows Indian fishing methods.

bows and arrows and traps to hunt the numerous bears, deer, wild turkeys, and other animals that lived in the forests. They made canoes by hollowing out tree trunks or by attaching tree bark to a wooden frame. They paddled their canoes out onto Maryland waters, where they caught fish with nets, spears, and even bows and arrows. Canoes were also an important means of transportation to the Native Americans.

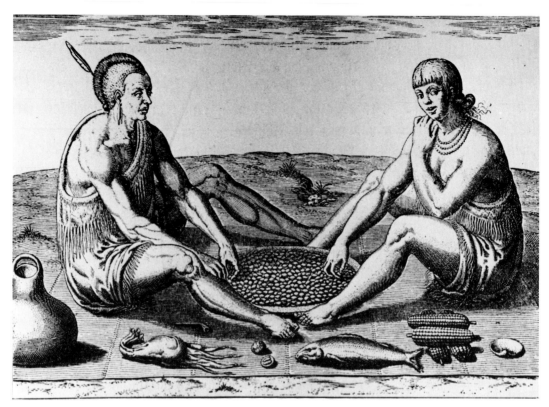

Indians raised corn and gathered nuts and berries.

Fish cooking on
a wooden rack

Women grew corn, beans, pumpkins, and other crops in fields near the village, and also gathered clams, oysters, nuts, strawberries, and raspberries with their children. The women were in charge of the cooking, too. Corn, which was used to make bread, stews, and a puffed-kernel dish called *hominy*, was the Indians' main food. Meat and fish stews were also popular.

Before the arrrival of Europeans, the Indians didn't wear much clothing. Children often went about naked—at least in warm weather. Adults usually wore a kind of apron that reached to the knees and was tied with a belt. Many Indians wore furs in winter. The Native Americans loved jewelry. They adorned themselves with necklaces, bracelets, and headbands made of animal teeth and shell beads. They also painted their faces and bodies with plant and mineral dyes. The Susquehannock reportedly painted green, red, black, and white stripes across their faces.

Chiefs, some of whom were women, guided the villages and tribes in their daily affairs. Special war captains directed the fighting when there were clashes with other tribes. The Nanticoke were greatly feared in wartime because of the poisonous substance they used on their arrow tips. Other tribes claimed that the Nanticoke could kill their enemies just by breathing on them—a belief that probably came from the Nanticokes' use of poisons.

Unlike the Europeans, the Indians did not believe in just one God. They honored many gods and spirits of the woods, sky, and water. It is thought that the Susquehannock believed in two main gods—one good and the other evil. They paid more attention to the evil god because they feared him so much. The Indians smoked tobacco while praying to their gods, in the belief that the

Indian man dressed for winter

19

smoke carried their prayers up to heaven. The Patuxent blew smoke over their entire bodies as part of their religious rites.

Although we know some facts about the beliefs of Maryland's Indians, we lack many details. There are two main reasons why we know less about Maryland's tribes than about Native Americans elsewhere. For one thing, some European authors of the 1600s exaggerated their reports. The Susquehannock, for example, were said to be a "giant-like people" whose men were "for the most part seven feet high." Studies of skeletons have shown that Susquehannock men averaged only about five feet four inches in height, which was about the average height of European men at that time. Such exaggerations cast doubt on other early reports concerning these Indians.

The other reason that we know so little about Maryland's Indians is that few of them were still around in the 1700s, when authors were writing a great deal about the Native Americans. In other colonies, authors could ask the Indians about their ancestors' customs. But Maryland's Indians had all but disappeared within several generations of the arrival of Europeans. Many of them were pushed out after selling their land to the colonists. Others died from diseases brought by

Indian woman

the Europeans, and some died in battles with the newcomers.

The Susquehannock are a tragic example of the total destruction of a tribe. After being pushed from place to place, only twenty Susquehannock people were alive by 1763. Around Christmas of that year, the last twenty Susquehannocks in the world were murdered by a mob in Pennsylvania.

It is believed that about 15,000 Indians lived in Maryland when the first Europeans arrived. Today the state has about 23,000 people of Indian heritage, but only about half of them are related to the region's original tribes. Many of the Indians who live in Maryland today belong to families that moved into the state from other places since colonial times. Maryland remembers its original Indians in some of its place names, including the Pocomoke, Nanticoke, Choptank, Patuxent, Wicomico, Potomac, and Susquehanna rivers.

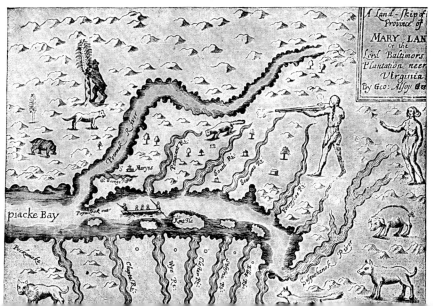

Maryland in 1666

Giovanni da Verrazano may have explored the coast of Maryland in his ship *Dauphine*. The route of Verrazano, who sailed from France, is shown on the map.

Chapter III

Exploration and First Settlement

This bay [Chesapeake Bay] is the most delightful water I ever saw, [and it is located] between two sweet lands.

From Relation of Maryland *(1635), by Father Andrew White*

The period from the late 1400s through the early 1600s is sometimes called the *Age of Discovery*. During those years, sailors from Portugal, Spain, Italy, France, England, and The Netherlands explored many parts of the world, including the Americas.

We do not know the identity of the first Europeans to reach what is now the United States. Some historians think that Vikings (Norwegians and other Scandinavians) reached the East Coast of what is now the United States around 1000 A.D. Other historians think that the first Europeans arrived in what is now the United States in the late 1400s or the early 1500s. As for the great Italian sailor Christopher Columbus, he never reached the present-day United States in 1492 or on any of his three later voyages. Instead, Columbus explored islands in the Caribbean Sea and parts of Central and South America.

The identity of the first explorer to reach what is now Maryland is also unknown. It may have been Giovanni da Verrazano (1485?–1528), an Italian navigator working for France. In early 1524, Verrazano sailed the *Dauphine* westward across the Atlantic Ocean. After reaching Cape Fear, North Carolina, around March 1, 1524, Verrazano is thought to have explored the Chincoteague Bay region where southeastern Maryland borders Virginia. He then sailed north to what is now the Canadian coast beyond Maine. Along the way, he became the first known European to explore the coasts of several states. Within a few years of Verrazano's trip, Spanish sailors were exploring Chesapeake Bay near present-day Virginia and Maryland.

However, English people—rather than the French or the Spanish—were the main colonizers of what became the United States. Permanent English settlement of America began in 1607 with the founding of Jamestown, Virginia, near the entrance to Chesapeake Bay. One of Jamestown's leaders was Captain John Smith, a man who fell

Giovanni da Verrazano

John Smith trading with the Indians.

in love with America. Captain Smith went on several expeditions from Jamestown. On one expedition that he made in 1607 he was captured by Indians and sentenced to die. His life was saved by Pocahontas, the daughter of Chief Powhatan.

In 1608, Captain Smith made two explorations of the Chesapeake Bay area. On the first trip he explored Maryland's Nanticoke, Pocomoke, and Potomac rivers, sailing up the Potomac as far as the spot where Washington, D.C., now stands.

Pocahontas

Just a few days after returning to Jamestown, Captain Smith went out to explore the Chesapeake Bay territory again. On this trip he reached the head of the bay in northeastern Maryland where he met some Susquehannock Indians. While returning to Virginia, he explored the Patapsco and Patuxent rivers on Maryland's Western Shore, including the spot on the Patapsco where Baltimore now stands.

Captain Smith's stories about the wonders of the Chesapeake Bay area helped attract English people to Virginia and Maryland. Within a few years, Englishmen were entering the Maryland region to trade trinkets and tools to the Indians in exchange for valuable furs. One of these men, Henry Spelman, traded peacefully with the Indians along the Potomac for several years. Unfortunately, Spelman was killed by Indians in 1623. He may have been killed because the Indians were angry at the English for taking their lands in Virginia.

William Claiborne

William Claiborne was another English trader who came to the Maryland region. After arriving in America in 1621, Claiborne worked as a public official in Virginia and traded for furs with Indians to the north. Around 1630, Claiborne sailed to England where he obtained permission to build a trading post in Chesapeake Bay. He and dozens of his followers returned to Chesapeake Bay in 1631. They settled a few miles east of present-day Annapolis on an island Claiborne named Kent. Claiborne's trading post on Kent Island is considered Maryland's first permanent English settlement.

Meanwhile George Calvert, an important public official in England, had become very interested in colonizing America. During the early 1620s, Calvert founded a colony in Newfoundland, Canada, that failed partly because of the cold climate. Then around 1625 Calvert left the Church of England (the country's official religion) became a Roman Catholic, and resigned from public office. At that time, English Catholics and other people who didn't belong to the Church of England were persecuted. Although King James I as head of the Church of England persecuted people for religious reasons, he liked George Calvert. In 1625 he gave Calvert the title *Lord Baltimore* as a gesture of friendship.*

King James I of England

By the late 1620s, George Calvert wanted to build a new colony far south of Newfoundland where English Catholics and other Christians of all beliefs could live in peace. In the summer of 1629 he wrote a letter to Charles I (who became

* See document on page 145

27

king of England in 1625) asking permission to found a new colony on Chesapeake Bay in the vicinity of Virginia. That same year Calvert sailed from Newfoundland to visit Virginia. Although he was insulted in Virginia because of his religion, Calvert was impressed by the region's rich soil, many rivers, and mild climate. It was reported that during this trip Calvert enjoyed watching and listening to the songbird that was later named the Baltimore oriole after him and the other Lords Baltimore.

After returning to England in late 1629, Calvert promoted his cause with the king. Charles I discouraged him, saying that new colonies often had "rugged and laborious beginnings." If anything, this was an understatement! Despite the glowing written reports of Captain John Smith and others, moving to the New World was a death sentence to most of the English people who tried it. For example, of the first 1,000 people who sailed to Jamestown after its founding in 1607, all but 60 died of disease, hunger, or other hardships within three years. And of the approximately 100 Pilgrims who founded Plymouth, Massachusetts, in 1620, about half were dead by the end of the first winter.

George Calvert didn't give up, though. He continued to petition the king and English lawmakers. At first he requested land in what is now southern Virginia, but Virginians wouldn't give up their land. Calvert then asked for a region north of the Potomac River that was a little larger than present-day Maryland. George Calvert was said to have written his colonial charter himself, leaving a blank where the king could fill in the colony's name.

Virginians opposed Calvert's plan, partly because they didn't want a Catholic colony as a neighbor. William Claiborne and his followers also opposed it because it meant that Kent Island would be within Calvert's domain. Nevertheless, King Charles I finally granted George Calvert's request, mainly because England wanted to rule the entire east coast. As of early 1632, the only English colonies along the coast were Virginia in the south and Massachusetts, Maine, and New Hampshire in the north. The founding of a colony just north of Virginia would give England another valuable piece of American real estate.

The king approved George Calvert's plan in the spring of 1632. Then came the fun part—choosing the colony's name. King Charles I decided to name

King Charles I and Queen Henrietta Maria

it after his wife, Queen Henrietta Maria. Reportedly the colony was nearly named *Mariana* before the king decided on *Terra Maria*, which is Latin for "Land of Maria." Later, the name was translated into English as the single word *Maryland.**

Tragically, George Calvert died on April 15, 1632, about two months before the official charter was granted. The charter was issued on June 20, 1632, to George Calvert's son, Cecil Calvert, the second Lord Baltimore. This charter was very generous to Cecil Calvert and his heirs, giving them almost the power of kings over the colony.

* See document describing Maryland on page 146

As Maryland's "Lord Proprietors," they would grant lands to people who would pay them rent. They would also receive money from various fees and duties paid on products going in and out of Maryland.

In accordance with his father's wishes, Cecil Calvert decreed that the people of Maryland would have a great deal of religious freedom for that era. Christians of all churches were to have equal rights in Maryland. This was in contrast to England, where many people who did not belong to the Church of England were stripped of their property, fired from their jobs, and jailed.

Cecil Calvert opened an office in London, England, and began signing up people who wanted to move to Maryland. Although some of them were Catholics, more than half belonged to Protestant churches. There were some families, but most were men who were sailing to America by themselves. And although a few were rich, most were farmers, laborers, and servants. Among those Maryland pioneers were several Catholic priests, including Father Andrew White, who later wrote *Relation of Maryland*, a work that tells us a great deal about the young colony.*

The approximately 150 people who were moving to Maryland left England on the *Ark* and the *Dove*

Cecil Calvert

* A page from a Father White's journal is shown on page 147

31

The first colonists sailed to Maryland on the *Ark* and the *Dove*.

in November 1633. The Lord Proprietor, Cecil Calvert, was not among them. He stayed in England to defend his claim to Maryland from anyone who might try to take it from him, and never did visit his colony. However, Cecil sent his brother, Leonard Calvert, to govern Maryland for him.

Why were those 150 pioneers willing to face the hardships and dangers of moving to a strange land just for the chance to live in Maryland? Many of them were seeking the religious freedom that was the main idea behind the founding of Maryland. Generally speaking, Europeans of the 1600s were much more religious than Europeans and Americans are today. Thousands of English people gladly risked and often lost their lives during the 1600s for the sake of worshiping as they chose. The English Pilgrims endured many hardships in Massachusetts after their arrival in 1620 for the sake of religious liberty.

However, some of the passengers had more practical reasons for moving to the New World. According to English laws of the time, the oldest son inherited most of his father's lands and property, leaving younger sons rather poor. The opportunity to acquire land had drawn many such men to Virginia, and now Cecil Calvert was luring many more to Maryland by offering them large tracts of land. Any man who paid his own way to Maryland would receive 100 acres. A man who paid the way of five other colonists would receive 2,000 acres.*

A number of the passengers hoped to find treasure in Maryland. Many Spanish people had grown wealthy from the gold and silver that they obtained from their colonies in Mexico and Peru. It was widely believed that the east coast of what is now the United States was rich in gold and silver deposits. Other people hoped to make their fortune by trading with the Indians for furs. Still others came out of a spirit of adventure or because they wanted to make a fresh start in life for one reason or another. As for the priests, they wanted

* For further information see document on page 148

to save the souls of the colonists and the Indians.

After a voyage of more than three months, the *Ark* and the *Dove* reached the mouth of Chesapeake Bay on February 27, 1634. First the newcomers stopped in Virginia, where they were greeted kindly (perhaps because the king had sent a letter with Governor Leonard Calvert *ordering* the Virginians to be friendly). After visiting Virginia, the Marylanders continued northward to their own new colony.

For several weeks, the colonists explored the area near the Potomac River in search of a site for their first town. On March 25, 1634, the priests held a thanksgiving Mass on St. Clements Island in the Potomac. This was the first Catholic Mass

Landing of Leonard Calvert at St. Mary's, 1634

in Maryland. Today, more than 350 years later, March 25 is still honored as Maryland Day.

Leonard Calvert had been instructed by his brother, Cecil, to establish friendly ties with the Indians. While exploring a little river near the Potomac that the colonists named the Saint Marys, Leonard Calvert met with the Yaocomico Indians—a peaceful people who were planning to abandon their village out of fear of the Susquehannock. On March 27, 1634, Governor Calvert made a deal with the Yaocomicos. The Indians would give their village and a few square miles of land around it to the colonists in exchange for some cloth, hatchets, and hoes. The Indians were to give up half their village immediately and the other half over the coming year. In this way, the colonists obtained wigwams for their first homes as well as farmland at a cheap price.

The newcomers fired cannons and flew their flags as they marched to their ready-made village. Governor Calvert named the town Saint Marys (which was later changed slightly to St. Marys City) in honor of the Virgin Mary and Queen Henrietta Maria. St. Marys City was to serve as the capital of the Maryland Colony for 60 years until 1694, when Annapolis became the seat of government.

GEORGE CALVERT (1580?-1632)

George Calvert

George Calvert was born into a wealthy family at Kipling, England, around 1580. At 14 he entered Oxford University where he studied Latin, French, Spanish, astronomy, and mathematics. After graduating from Oxford at about the age of 17 he went on a European tour during which he learned to speak and write French, Spanish, and Italian very well. While in France he met Sir Robert Cecil, England's secretary of state (a position somewhat like that of prime minister in modern Great Britain).

Sir Robert Cecil was impressed by George's knowledge of languages, and in 1606 he hired him as a translator and aide. While working for Sir Robert Cecil, George Calvert won the respect of King James I, who helped him with his political career. In 1609 George Calvert was elected to Parliament, the English lawmaking body, and in 1619 the king made George Calvert the secretary of state, the post Sir Robert Cecil had held before his death in 1612.

George Calvert and his first wife, Anne Mynne, had 11 children, including Cecil and Leonard. It may have been Anne's death in 1622 that prompted George Calvert to leave the Church of England and become a Catholic. Because of England's laws against Catholics, Calvert resigned as secretary of state, but received the title of Lord Baltimore from King James I as a token of friendship.

Calvert was keenly interested in American colonization, and in the 1620s he sent settlers to build a colony called Avalon in Newfoundland, Canada. He visited Avalon in 1627 and again from 1628 to 1629 to find out why the colony was doing so poorly, despite his having spent a fortune on it. By this time, Calvert had a pressing reason for establishing a successful American colony. He wanted to build a place where Catholics and other persecuted people could live in peace.

Calvert saw that Newfoundland's cold climate was contributing to the failure of Avalon. He wrote the following letter from Avalon in the summer of 1629 asking King Charles I to grant him a colony in the Virginia region:

Avalon, August 19, 1629

Most gracious and dread Sovereign:

Your Majesty may please to understand . . . that from the middle of October to the middle of May there is a sad face of winter upon all this land. . . . My house hath been a hospital all this winter. Of a hundred persons, fifty [were] sick at a time, myself being one. I am determined to commit this place to fishermen that are better able to encounter storms and

*hard weather, and to remove myself with some 40 persons to your
Majesty's dominion, Virginia, where, if your Majesty will please to grant me
a precinct of land, with such privileges as the King, your father . . . was
pleased to grant me here, I shall endeavor, to the utmost of my power, to
deserve it and pray for your Majesty's long and happy reign.*

Your Majesty's most humble and faithful servant,

George Baltimore

Soon after writing this letter, Calvert sailed south from Avalon to
Virginia. He loved what he saw of Chesapeake Bay, and after returning to
England in late 1629 he spent the last two years of his life convincing the
king to grant him territory in the region. It was said that, even though
Calvert allowed the king to fill in the blank for the colony's name, he
himself favored the name *Crescentia*, a Latin word meaning "Land of
Increase." Maryland's "founding father" died at about the age of 52, just
66 days before the colony's official charter was issued, but his oldest son,
Cecil, carried out his dream.

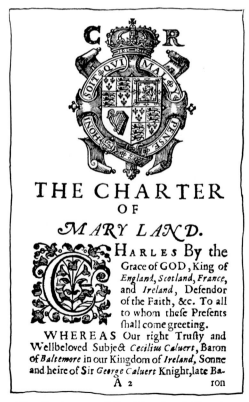

The first page of the Maryland Charter

The Baltimore coat of arms

Leonard Calvert establishing
the first settlement
in Maryland

Chapter IV

When Maryland Was Young: 1634–1689

... The land [around St. Marys City] is good, the air wholesome and pleasant, the river affords a safe harbor for ships of any burden, and [there is] a very bold shore. Fresh water and wood there is in great plenty, and the place so naturally fortified, as with little difficulties it will be defended from any enemy.

Father Andrew White, describing the site of St. Marys City in Relation of Maryland *(1635)*

The *Dove*

Maryland's Lord Proprietor, Cecil Calvert, had scheduled the voyage of the *Ark* and the *Dove* so that his colonists would arrive in time for the spring planting. During that spring of 1634, the newcomers planted corn and other crops in the fields that the Indians had provided. While living in the Indians' wigwams, they began building a storehouse, a big fort, and English-style cottages.

Although later colonists pushed the Indians off their lands, relations were good at St. Marys City between the Native Americans and the settlers.

The Indians showed the colonists how to make corn bread, hominy, potatoes baked in ashes, and other Indian dishes. They sold the newcomers log canoes and fishing nets, and taught them how to make these things for themselves.

The colonists at St. Marys City did not suffer from the "starving time" that had killed so many people at Jamestown, Virginia. Besides the food that they grew themselves and obtained from the Indians, they shot wild turkeys, ducks, geese, elk, and deer in the nearby woods, and obtained crabs, oysters, fish, and terrapins (a kind of turtle) in nearby waters.

St. Marys City never grew into a large colonial town like Boston in Massachusetts, New Amsterdam (now New York City) in New York, or Philadelphia in Pennsylvania. In fact, colonial Maryland never had a big city. Instead, people for the most part fanned out across the countryside on farms of various sizes. This was the general pattern throughout the Southern colonies, with the exception of Charleston in South Carolina.

The Maryland charter provided that the colony have a government, called the General Assembly, with limited power. (Maryland's legislature is still called the General Assembly, only it has much more power today.) The first General Assembly

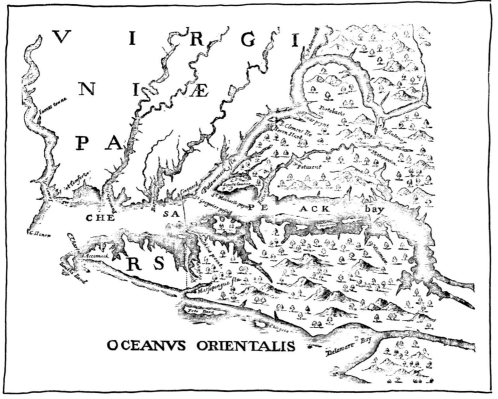

Map of Maryland drawn in 1635

that met at St. Marys City on February 26, 1635 acted rebellious just by passing laws. When sent to England for approval, these laws were rejected by Lord Baltimore, who reminded the Marylanders of an important point. According to Maryland's charter, he alone had the right to make laws. In turn, the General Assembly rejected some laws Lord Baltimore sent over from England. After crossing the ocean and building homes and towns on their own, the Marylanders (like many people in other colonies) resented being told what to do by an English ruler 3,000 miles away.

Finally, in the summer of 1638, Lord Baltimore agreed that the General Assembly could suggest laws that would not take effect until they were approved by Maryland's governor. Since the governor was his brother Leonard, this didn't seem very threatening to the Lord Proprietor.

More dangerous threats were coming from William Claiborne. Lord Baltimore maintained that Kent Island was part of Maryland and that Claiborne could either pay him rent like other Marylanders or move. Claiborne, however, claimed that his settlement was independent of Maryland. He continued trading for furs with the Indians without paying Lord Baltimore a cent.

William Claiborne's trading post on Kent Island

Claiborne and Calvert fought a sea battle over the status of Kent Island.

The situation came to a head when Claiborne sent a small ship to trade with the Indians only about ten miles from St. Marys City. An armed party sent out by Governor Calvert captured Claiborne's boat, men, and trade goods. Claiborne's men were locked in the St. Marys City jail.

Claiborne sought revenge by seizing a Maryland boat and by sending out a boat called the *Cockatrice* to fight the Marylanders. On April 23, 1635, two Maryland vessels, the *St. Helen* and the *St. Margaret*, fought the *Cockatrice* at the spot where the Pocomoke River empties into Chesapeake Bay on the Eastern Shore. Three of Claiborne's men were killed and the *Cockatrice* had to surrender in what is considered the first sea battle fought on Chesapeake Bay.

Nearly three years later, in early 1638, twenty armed men sent by Governor Calvert seized Kent Island without a fight. To make things worse for Claiborne, authorities in England informed him that Kent Island belonged to Maryland. William Claiborne felt that he had been robbed of the island, but fifteen years passed before he could do something about it.

Gradually, more English people moved to Maryland from England and Virginia, but the colony's early growth was very slow. Malaria and other diseases claimed many lives. By the early 1640s, at least one-fifth of the colonists who had moved to Maryland were dead. Only about 500 colonists lived in or near St. Marys City.

People who had hoped to grow rich from mining gold and silver in Maryland were of course disappointed. Those who had hoped the fur trade would make them rich didn't do much better. Fur-bearing animals were less abundant in Maryland than they were elsewhere. For most people, Maryland's two main attractions proved to be religious freedom and tobacco.

In 1649, Maryland's General Assembly approved the Act Concerning Religion, which had been suggested by Cecil Calvert, the second Lord Baltimore. This law guaranteed religious freedom for all Christians and set fines for people who made religious slurs.* Assurance of religious liberty attracted more people to Maryland, including about 300 Puritans who came from Virginia the year the act was passed. The Puritans had opposed the Church of England on many issues and hoped to "purify" or improve it. The Puritans founded a community called Providence, which included modern-day Annapolis, at the place where the Severn River empties into Chesapeake Bay. By 1650, Maryland's colonial population had climbed to about 4,500.

As for tobacco, there had been a demand for the American-grown crop ever since the Virginian John Rolfe had sent some tobacco leaves to England in 1613. Although Marylanders also grew corn, wheat, oats, and other food crops, tobacco soon was far and away the colony's number one product. By 1660, about 8,000 people lived in Maryland—mainly along the rivers that empty into Chesapeake Bay—and nearly all of them grew tobacco.

Philip Calvert, secretary of the General Assembly, endorsed the Act Concerning Religion.

* See document on page 149

Belle Air, one of the Maryland tobacco plantation mansions

Some rich tobacco planters built farms of 1,000 acres or more. We call these huge farms *plantations*, but back in the 1600s in Maryland they were called *manors*. The owners of these huge estates often gave them interesting names, such as Cornwalleys' Cross (built in 1643), Calvert's Rest (home of Governor Leonard Calvert's son), and Mulberry Grove.

The large plantations were built near rivers so that oceangoing ships could come right up to the wharves and load the tobacco. When the ships arrived from England, the plantation owners traded a portion of their tobacco for clothing, furniture, and other items. In this way, the plantation families were able to live much like wealthy people in England.

Much of the work on the plantations was done by what were called *indentured servants*. These were poor people whose passage to the New World had been paid by well-to-do colonists. In return, the indentured servants had to work for these colonists for about four years. Most indentured servants were male and about 17 years old when they arrived. They worked about 12 hours a day, six days a week. Indentured servants who disobeyed their masters could be beaten, and there were very harsh penalties for running away.

The life of an indentured servant wasn't without hope, though. Once they finished their term of service, indentured servants were freed and given new clothes, tools, a gun, and a tract of land. By the mid-1600s, almost half of all Marylanders were either indentured servants or former indentured servants. Many of them eventually achieved positions of importance, and some became wealthy planters themselves.

Indentured servants worked on the plantations.

Indentured servants willingly traded a few years of hard work for the chance to better themselves. But, starting in the 1640s, people began arriving in Maryland who had not chosen to move there. These were slaves. Although Maryland didn't have large-scale slavery until the 1700s, by 1660 about 1,000 of the 8,000 Marylanders were slaves.

Slaves working on a tobacco plantation

The slaves had a much harder life than the indentured servants. Not only were they forced to labor like work animals from sunrise to sunset, they couldn't look forward to the day when they would be free. Slaves nearly always remained slaves for life, and their children were also slaves.

By the late 1600s, though, fewer than one-third of all white Marylanders owned even one slave. Small and midsize farmers greatly outnumbered the plantation owners, and most of these people couldn't afford slaves. In fact, many of them had been indentured servants just a few years earlier.

An old plantation slave cabin

As first, the small and midsized farmers usually built simple wooden houses, and made their own furniture. They made bowls and cups from dried gourds, carved pieces of wood into spoons, and also made their own soap, candles, and clothing.

Sometimes two single men would run a farm together. Later, when more women arrived in Maryland, both men might marry. The two families might live together, or one of the men might build a new home for himself and his bride.

As soon as they could afford it, small and midsized farmers built brick houses. The old wooden house might serve as a barn or be used as a home for an indentured servant if the farmer could afford one. Instead of building a new home, some farmers kept adding onto their old homes as their families grew. Because such homes bulged out at the sides like a collapsible spyglass, they were called "telescope houses."

Many small and midsized farms were given humorous names, such as Bread and Cheese Hall, Hard Bargain, Charley, Bachelor's Hope, and Shepherd's Delight. Philip Key, great-grandfather of Francis Scott Key, lived in a brick house called Bushwood Lodge near Maryland's Wicomico River.

Tobacco dominated nearly every aspect of life in early Maryland. Since little money was in circulation, people used tobacco as money. Tobacco was used to buy goods and to pay rents, debts, court fees, and taxes. Land was bought with tobacco, estates were valued in the number of pounds of tobacco they were worth, and hired laborers were paid about 15 pounds of tobacco a day. Since ministers were paid in tobacco, people complained that areas with poor tobacco couldn't get good preachers!

While many Marylanders were becoming wealthy by growing tobacco, the colony was suffering from political turmoil. William Claiborne took part in a revolt against Maryland's government from 1644 to 1646. A Marylander named Margaret Brent organized troops to help Governor

Calvert put down this rebellion. Soon after this uprising ended, the governor became very ill. Just before his death in June 1647, Calvert named Thomas Greene, a well-known Catholic, as the next governor.

Meanwhile, major changes were occurring 3,000 miles away in England. During the 1640s, Puritans seized control of the British government. In 1649, King Charles I was beheaded, and from that year until 1660 England had no king or queen. Instead, the country was run by Oliver Cromwell and other Puritans. This affected the American Colonies because England's Puritans wanted the colonies to have Puritan governments too.

By 1649, Catholics in Maryland were outnumbered about 3 to 1 by the Puritans and other Protestants. Lord Baltimore apparently felt that if he gave the Protestants more power in Maryland, the Puritans might leave his colony alone. He removed Thomas Greene as governor in 1649 and replaced him with William Stone, a Protestant. Lord Baltimore also gave some other important government posts to Protestants. Even the Act Concerning Religion of 1649 had some political motives. Lord Baltimore hoped that ensuring the rights of Protestant Marylanders would prevent the Protestants from trying to deprive the

Catholics of their rights. These measures did not succeed, however.

In the early 1650s, Puritan lawmakers in England appointed commissioners, including the Calverts' old enemy William Claiborne, to help set up a Puritan government in Maryland. In 1654, Maryland's General Assembly, which by then was dominated by Puritans, declared that the colony was no longer Lord Baltimore's. William Claiborne helped create a system by which Maryland's government was run by a handful of Puritan commissioners. Lord Baltimore's forces fought back and for a short time there was a civil war in Maryland.

On March 24–25, 1655, about 100 of Lord Baltimore's men battled Puritan forces near Maryland's Severn River not far from present-day Annapolis. Aiding the Puritans was an armed ship, the *Golden Lion*, which fired its guns at the enemy. Most of Lord Baltimore's troops were killed, wounded, or captured, though a few escaped by swimming a creek and then running through the woods. Several of Lord Baltimore's men who were captured were hanged from trees after this Battle of the Severn.

The Puritans who ran Maryland for the next four years ended the religious freedom granted by

Governor Stone's forces were defeated by the Puritans.

the Act Concerning Religion of 1649. They said that Catholics couldn't practice their faith or even expect protection under Maryland's laws.

Cecil Calvert had made a wise choice by remaining in England to defend his right to Maryland. He tried to convince Oliver Cromwell and other Puritan leaders that Maryland should be restored to him. Calvert succeeded in late 1657 and, by early 1658, Maryland was once more under his control. The Act Concerning Religion went back into effect. In fact, soon after Maryland was restored to him, Lord Baltimore ended the persecution of Dr. Jacob Lumbrozo, a Jewish Marylander. Dr. Lumbrozo was to have stood trial for stating the Jewish belief that Jesus was not the son of God.

Charles Calvert

In 1661, Cecil Calvert appointed his son, Charles, to govern Maryland. Unlike his father and grandfather, Charles Calvert lived in Maryland for about 20 years. His home, St. John's Freehold, was in St. Marys City, the Maryland capital. Sandwiched around a trip to England, Charles Calvert governed Maryland from 1661 to 1676 and from 1679 until he returned to England in 1684. These were years of growth and prosperity for Maryland. One of Governor Charles Calvert's main achievements was organizing the Eastern Shore, which had been settled after the Western Shore, into separate counties. By 1674 Maryland had ten counties (today there are twenty-three), all on or very close to Chesapeake Bay. The counties were St. Marys, Anne Arundel, Calvert, Charles, and Baltimore on the Western Shore; Kent, Talbot, Somerset, and Dorchester on the Eastern Shore; and Cecil at the top of Chesapeake Bay. Each county was allowed to elect four delegates to the General Assembly.

Charles's father, Cecil Calvert, the second Lord Baltimore, died in 1675, having worked to establish and defend his colony for more than 40 years without ever visiting it. Charles Calvert then became the third Lord Baltimore and Maryland's Lord Proprietor and governor.

Just as the Puritan takeover in England had caused problems for his father in the 1650s, events in the mother country brought on a crisis for Charles Calvert. In 1688 James II, the Catholic king of England, was overthrown by his own daughter, Mary, and her husband William. William and Mary, who were Protestants, became king and queen in 1689.

When they learned that James II was no longer king, people in Boston, Massachusetts, seized Sir Edmund Andros, a friend of James's who had been appointed to govern Massachusetts and nearby colonies. Andros was sent back to England. In Maryland, the overthrow of the Catholic king convinced many Protestants that they could overthrow the Catholic Calvert family.

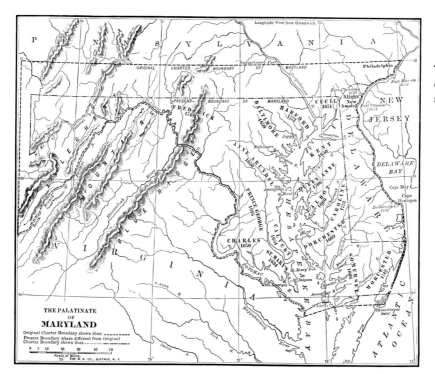

This map shows the dates of the early settlements.

In the summer of 1689, Protestants in Maryland organized the "Protestant Association," which was dedicated to toppling the Calverts. Under their leader John Coode, a former clergyman who had become a planter, 250 Protestant Association men marched toward St. Marys City in July 1689. The Calvert government surrendered without a fight.

The Protestant Association wanted Maryland to change from a proprietary colony (one privately owned) into a royal colony (one ruled directly by the monarch). The Protestant Association sent a letter to King William and Queen Mary asking that Maryland be made into a royal colony. The king and queen agreed, and Maryland became a royal colony in late 1689.

Charles Calvert, the third Lord Baltimore, was allowed to keep his lands and continue collecting rents, fees, and duties in Maryland. But he was stripped of political power. During Maryland's 26 years as a royal colony, its governors were appointed by England's monarchs.

CECIL CALVERT (About 1606–1675)

While climbing the political ladder, George Calvert worked as an official in Ireland, which was then under English rule. He accumulated a great deal of land in Ireland, and even his title *Lord Baltimore* was Irish. George and Anne Calvert's first son may have been born during their brief stay in Ireland. The couple named him Cecil for Sir Robert Cecil, the man who did so much to help George Calvert's career.

Like his father, Cecil Calvert attended Oxford University, but apparently he did not graduate. Around the age of 22, Cecil married Anne Arundel, the daughter of an English nobleman. About four years later George Calvert died, and as his oldest son, Cecil automatically became the second Lord Baltimore.

Cecil Calvert, second Lord Baltimore

Cecil Calvert had the difficult task of planning and carrying out the colonization of Maryland. He recruited settlers and arranged for the *Ark* and the *Dove* to take them to Maryland. A great deal of Cecil Calvert's own money went into that first voyage.

Cecil Calvert supported his father's idea of making Maryland a haven for all types of Christians. He was responsible for the Act Concerning Religion, the law that tried to eliminate religious prejudice among Christian Marylanders. Certain events in Maryland disturbed Cecil Calvert, though. He was upset that Marylanders demanded more say in their government, and amazed that they let a woman, Margaret Brent, have so much responsibility. Yet he was wise enough to back down on many issues and let Marylanders decide things for themselves, which helped the colony grow.

Cecil Calvert had hoped to visit Maryland soon after the *Ark* and the *Dove* left England, but he couldn't go then or at any other time during his more than 40 remaining years of life. England's monarchs could not be trusted to leave the American Colonies alone. They might suddenly cancel a colony's charter, change its boundaries, or even give it to someone else. Cecil Calvert stayed in England to protect his ownership of Maryland, and he did a good job. Despite a couple of interruptions, Maryland remained a Calvert possession for well over a century. Cecil Calvert died in London, England, at about the age of 69. Maryland's Cecil County was named for him, and Anne Arundel County was named for his wife.

MARGARET BRENT (About 1600-1671)

Margaret Brent was born into a prominent family in the city of Gloucester in southwestern England. In Margaret's time, women in England had few rights. They could not attend college, hold public office, or vote. They were excluded from law, the military, and most other professions. It was even considered wicked for a woman to live alone. Instead, females were supposed to live under the supervision of their fathers, husbands, or brothers. During her lifetime, Margaret Brent broke—or tried to break—all of these rules except the one concerning college. She might have fought that one, too, if there had been a college in Maryland.

Margaret apparently was very well educated in England, but we don't know much about her life before she came to America. When she reached her mid-30s, Margaret heard about the Maryland Colony that the Calverts had founded as a religious haven. Margaret and her family were Catholics. She, her sister Mary, and their brothers Giles and Fulke decided to move to Maryland. They sailed from England in late 1638 and arrived at St. Marys City in 1639.

In the fall of 1639, Margaret Brent was granted about 70 acres at St. Marys City, making her Maryland's first female landowner. She and Mary lived on this land and called it the "Sisters' Freehold." Margaret and Mary had also paid for the passage of a few other colonists. According to the Calverts' rules at that time the sisters were entitled to more land—about 1,000 acres—for having done this. After a few years of fighting for it, the sisters finally received title to this land. Margaret kept transporting colonists to Maryland and thus became one of the colony's largest landowners, female or male.

Before William Claiborne took part in seizing Maryland's government in 1654, he participated in an unsuccessful revolt from 1644 to 1646. Margaret Brent organized troops that helped Governor Leonard Calvert put down this rebellion. Just before he died in June 1647, Leonard Calvert named Margaret Brent to oversee his will and personal affairs. "Take all and pay all," the dying governor told her, meaning that she should collect all money due him and pay all his debts.

In carrying out the governor's will, Margaret Brent faced one very big problem. Leonard Calvert had promised that he would personally pay the troops who had helped him put down the rebellion, but he hadn't left enough money. A crisis seemed to be at hand when the soldiers threatened to revolt unless they were paid. Margaret Brent then took it upon herself to sell some of Lord Proprietor Cecil Calvert's property and use the money to pay the troops.

Cecil Calvert was angry when word reached England that Margaret Brent had sold his property without asking him. But the Maryland Assembly approved Margaret Brent's actions and informed Cecil Calvert that she had helped save his colony. The Assembly even appointed Margaret Brent as Cecil Calvert's lawyer in Maryland, making her the first female lawyer in America. This meant that she collected Lord Baltimore's rents and managed his Maryland property.

Perhaps it was all these responsibilities that planted what was then considered an outlandish idea in Margaret Brent's head. In early 1648 she asked to be admitted as a member of the all-male General Assembly. She even claimed that she deserved *two* votes in the General Assembly—one as a large Maryland landowner and the second as the Lord Proprietor's lawyer. The prospect of women voting or holding public office was unheard of in those days.

Thomas Greene, who became governor on Leonard Calvert's death, turned down Margaret Brent's request to enter the General Assembly. This—and the fact that Cecil Calvert was still angry at her for selling his property—prompted Margaret Brent to move to an estate she called "Peace" on the Virginia side of the Potomac River in 1650. "America's First Feminist," as she is sometimes called, lived there for 21 years, until her death at about the age of 71.

The document that appointed Thomas Greene governor of Maryland

The old state house (right) was
built at St. Marys City in 1676
Annapolis in 1710

Chapter V

The Royal Colony: 1689-1715

We have thought fit to take our Province of Maryland under our immediate care and protection.

> *From a statement by Queen Mary around the time that Maryland became a royal colony*

King William appointed Sir Lionel Copley as Maryland's first royal governor in 1691, and Sir Lionel took office the next year. As had occurred during the Puritan takeover of the 1650s, freedom of religion all but vanished from Maryland. In June 1692, under Royal Governor Copley's direction, the General Assembly named the Church of England (now called the Episcopal Church in the United States) as Maryland's official religion. Everyone—whether Church of Englanders, Catholics, Quakers, or Jews—had to pay a yearly tax of 40 pounds of tobacco to help support the Church of England. That same year, Maryland's ten counties were divided into separate Church of England parishes (church districts).

Although Catholics could still practice their religion at home, Catholic priests were forbidden to say masses or hold baptisms. In 1704, Catholics were forbidden to have their own parochial schools and to convert people to their religion. A few years later, Catholic lawyers were barred from practicing in Maryland, and Catholics were deprived of the right to vote. Not until after colonial times ended did Maryland have the kind of religious freedom it had offered at its founding in the 1630s.

However, some good things did happen during the 26 years of royal rule. In the late 1680s, a man named William Nuthead became Maryland's first printer when he set up a press at St. Marys City. Nuthead worked as a printer for the royal government. After William's death in 1694, his widow, Dinah Nuthead, took over his press and thus became the first known female printer in the colonies. However, Dinah Nuthead moved the press northward to be near the new Maryland capital—Annapolis.

St. Marys City had not grown into the thriving town that early Marylanders had hoped it would become. It was really just a bunch of houses and public buildings sprawled out over a few miles.

The early settlements were near Chesapeake Bay. Land travel between the settlements was difficult because of the poor roads.

Maryland's cities

Besides not being much of a town, St. Marys City was located at Maryland's southern tip and was hard to reach over the poor roads and the many rivers that had to be crossed. By the early 1690s, many Marylanders favored a change of capital.

In 1694, Francis Nicholson became Maryland's royal governor. One of Governor Nicholson's first decisions was to move Maryland's capital to Anne Arundel Town on the Severn River. The name of the small settlement was soon changed from Anne Arundel Town to Annapolis. *Polis* is an ancient Greek word meaning "city," so Annapolis means *city of Anne*. The name honored Princess Anne, who later ruled Great Britain as Queen Anne between 1702 and 1714.

The people in St. Marys City fought to keep the capital. They even offered to provide coaches for some people who had trouble reaching their town. But they lost this battle. By the end of 1694 Annapolis was officially Maryland's capital—an honor it has held ever since. Of the 50 U.S. state capitals, only Santa Fe, New Mexico (since 1610); Boston, Massachusetts (since 1630); and Providence, Rhode Island (since 1663), have served as colonial and then state capitals longer than Annapolis. In 1994 Annapolis will celebrate its

The old capitol at Annapolis

300th anniversary as the Maryland capital.

During the period of royal rule, progress was also made in providing education and books for Marylanders. Until the 1690s, Maryland had no public schools. The children of rich Marylanders were taught by private tutors who were often indentured servants from England. Other children were taught by their ministers, by their parents, or not at all. Old documents reveal that half the men in early colonial Maryland couldn't read or write. We know this because they made marks on the documents instead of signing their names. The percentage of women who couldn't read or write was of course higher, because girls received less schooling than boys in those days.

Although Maryland's public school system didn't really get going until the 1800s, the seeds for public education were planted in 1694. That year the General Assembly passed a law that school funds be provided from duties on furs and skins shipped out of Maryland. This was clearly a half-hearted attempt at raising money for education. Had the lawmakers been really serious, the money would have been raised from their much larger tobacco exports. This act did lead to the establishment of Maryland's first free school,

A hornbook used in the colonial schools. Paper was scarce and expensive, so the lessons were pasted to a wooden board and protected by a thin sheet of horn.

Thomas Bray

however. Called King William's School, it was founded in Annapolis in 1696 for the purpose of teaching Latin, Greek, writing, and religion to young men. Nearly 100 years later, this academy became St. John's College, which is still operating in Annapolis.

A short time after King William's School was founded, the first libraries were set up in Maryland. They were the brainchild of Thomas Bray, a Church of England minister. Reverend Bray collected money in England for books that he shipped to Maryland in the late 1690s. Bray finally came to Maryland himself around the year 1700 and set up 30 parish libraries in the colony.

While in Maryland, Reverend Bray also helped supply many parishes with Church of England ministers.

Transportation and communication also improved during Maryland's 26 years of royal rule. In 1695, Maryland's first postal route was established. It started along the Potomac River in the Saint Marys City region, went north through the capital city of Annapolis, and continued northeast all the way to Philadelphia, Pennsylvania. A person could then send a letter from the Potomac River area to Philadelphia—about 200 miles—in about two weeks. Today this would be considered much too slow, but it was pretty good three centuries ago!

St. George Island near the mouth of the Potomac River

Laying out Baltimore town, January 12, 1780

Chapter VI

A Proprietary Colony Again: 1715–1760s

. . . Port Annapolis,
the famous Beau Metropolis
of Maryland, of small Renown
When Anna first wore England's Crown,
Is now Grown Rich and Opulent
The awful Seat of Government.

Description of Annapolis, from a poem
written by Ebenezer Cook in 1730

Charles Calvert, the third Lord Baltimore, died in 1715 at the age of 77. Because of his refusal to forsake the Catholic Church, he never regained political power in Maryland. Upon Charles Calvert's death, his son, Benedict Leonard Calvert, became the fourth Lord Baltimore and Maryland's Lord Proprietor.

For most of his life, Benedict Leonard Calvert belonged to the Catholic Church, like his father (Charles Calvert), grandfather (Cecil Calvert), and great-grandfather (George Calvert) before him. But in late 1713, Benedict Leonard Calvert renounced Catholicism, joined the Church of England, and had his children do the same.

George I

George I, who became king of Great Britain in 1714, was pleased that Benedict Leonard Calvert had given up Catholicism, as were other English officials. When Benedict Leonard Calvert asked George I to restore Maryland to him, the king agreed. In 1715, Maryland again became a proprietary colony under the Calverts and remained so until the Revolutionary War 60 years later.

By 1715—the year it was returned to the Calverts—Maryland had a few small towns, all of them on or close to Chesapeake Bay. The Western Shore towns at that time included St. Marys City (founded in 1634), Annapolis (1649), Port Tobacco (mid-1600s), and Leonardtown (1708). Eastern Shore towns included Elkton (founded in 1672), Cambridge (1684), Easton (late 1600s), and Chestertown (about 1700).

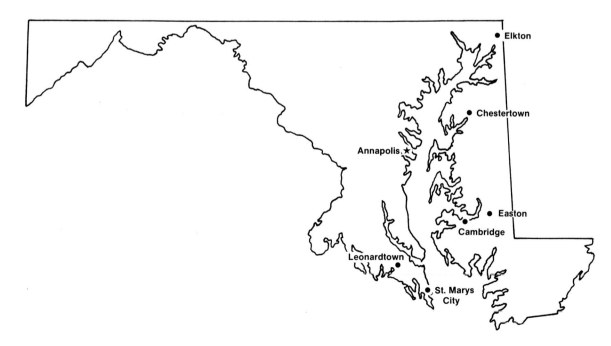

The years between 1715 and 1760 were years of great growth in Maryland, as they were in all the colonies. During that time, Maryland's population more than tripled from around 50,000 people (slightly less than the Baltimore Orioles' home stadium holds today) to about 160,000. By 1760, the only colonies with more people than Maryland were Virginia (340,000), Massachusetts (223,000), and Pennsylvania (184,000). Maryland's population growth was partly due to the high birthrate—families often had ten or twelve children in colonial times. And it was partly due to the thousands of people who poured into Maryland from England, Germany, Ireland, Scotland, France, Italy, The Netherlands, and other parts of colonial America in the hope of making a fortune by growing tobacco.

The most striking population change was the rise in the number of black slaves. Until about 1690, Maryland was home to many more indentured servants than slaves, because slaves were very expensive. However, Maryland's farmers were discovering advantages in owning slaves, even if they had to borrow money to buy them. After a few years, the indentured servants were free, while slaves and their children remained the planters' property for life and also rose in value over time.

Slave traders loading their cargo in Africa

By the early 1700s, slaves outnumbered indentured servants in Maryland, and soon there were many more slaves than indentured servants in the colony. By 1760, nearly one-third of all Marylanders were slaves. About half of Maryland's white families owned at least one slave, and a few wealthy planters owned more than 100 slaves.

Maryland's population growth led to the founding of new towns. By the 1720s, some people had settled near the spot where the Patapsco River flows into the west side of Chesapeake Bay. The local farmers wanted to have a town where they could store their tobacco and then export it.

In the summer of 1729, the Maryland General Assembly bought 60 acres of land at the mouth of the Patapsco for the purpose of founding a town. The new town was named Baltimore in honor of the Calvert family. Despite its great harbor, Baltimore grew slowly at first, and had only about 200 residents as late as the 1750s. Not until the late 1700s, when flour milling became important, did Baltimore start to grow into the city that is now one of the twelve most populous cities in the United States.

Baltimore in 1752

One problem facing people who came to Maryland in the 1700s was that most of the prime farmland along the Chesapeake Bay rivers was already claimed. This prompted some people to move to the frontier west of Baltimore and build farms and towns there. The Calverts had a special reason for wanting to fill Maryland's unsettled areas. For much of colonial times, the Calverts quarreled over Maryland's boundaries with neighbors, especially the Penn family who were the proprietors of Pennsylvania. The more of Maryland that was settled, the better were the Calverts' chances of holding onto all of their territory.

People from Germany led the settlement of western Maryland. The first Germans had reached Maryland in 1684. In 1732 the Calverts made an offer that drew many more Germans to western Maryland from both Pennsylvania and Europe. Any man who settled his family in a large region west of Baltimore could have 200 acres for a small rental fee. Any single person between the ages of 15 and 30 could have 100 acres. This meant that a couple with a few teenage children could have a large tract of wilderness land for very little money.

During the 1730s, about 100 German families led by John Thomas Schley settled in an area about 50 miles northwest of Baltimore. The town they helped build there was named Frederick, perhaps for Frederick Calvert, the sixth Lord Baltimore. Within a generation or so, Frederick rivaled Annapolis in population.

Another German immigrant, Jonathan Hager, settled in the wilderness about 75 miles northwest of Baltimore in the late 1730s. Hager, who obtained about four square miles of land in this region, built a log home for himself and sold lots for a new town. Hager called the town Elizabeth, for his wife, but most people called it Hagerstown and that became its official name in the early 1800s.

In 1747, a group of wealthy London merchants and Virginians founded the First Ohio Company. Its goals were to settle the lands near the Ohio River and to make sure that France didn't take over the region. In 1750, the First Ohio Company built a trading post and storehouse about 45 miles from Maryland's western edge. This outpost grew into the town of Cumberland.

One of the land disputes that the Calverts had with the Penns concerned Delaware. Both families wanted Delaware as part of their colony. The Penns won this dispute, and for most of colonial times Delaware was part of Pennsylvania. Another

The boundary dispute between Maryland, Pennsylvania, and Delaware was settled in 1732. The settlement was made on the basis of this map, which misrepresents the location of Cape Henlopen. The mistake cost Maryland about 15 miles along what is now the southern border of Delaware.

dispute with the Penns concerned Maryland's northern border with Pennsylvania. A Maryland frontiersman named Thomas Cresap became famous for his rough-and-ready ways of dealing with this conflict.

In 1729, Maryland granted Cresap a piece of land near what is now Columbia, Pennsylvania. Officials in Pennsylvania claimed that this was their land and that Cresap and other Marylanders who moved there were trespassers. Thomas Cresap started a border war against Pennsylvanians that involved raids on farms and even some shooting. Pennsylvania officials finally decided to attack the "Maryland Monster," as they called Cresap. In 1736 they burned down his house, forcing him and his family to flee. Cresap was captured and taken in chains all the way to Philadelphia, Pennsylvania.

Crowds of Philadelphians gathered just to get a look at Cresap, who was said to be a giant of a man. When the Philadelphians heckled him, Cresap reportedly said: "Damn it, this [Philadelphia] is one of the prettiest towns in Maryland!" Cresap was later released and in 1741 he founded Oldtown, Maryland, near Cumberland. As for the fight over the Maryland-Pennsylvania border, that wasn't settled until the 1760s when the famous Mason-Dixon line was drawn to resolve the issue. Maryland didn't get the land it wanted and of course Philadelphia remained part of Pennsylvania.

The map shows the Mason-Dixon line. Limestone markers (above) were set up along the line.

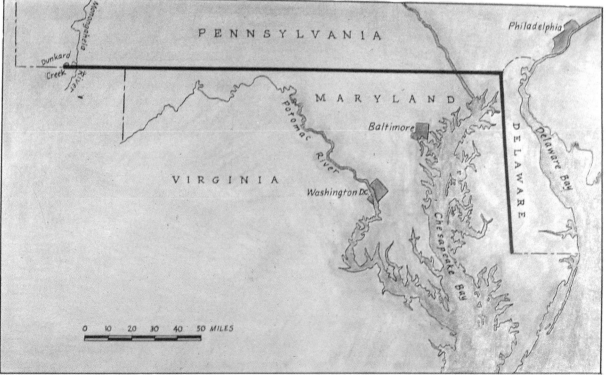

While the Marylanders and Pennsylvanians were arguing, there was also trouble from another country—France. The French ruled part of Canada, which they called New France, to the north of England's thirteen colonies. France and England wanted each other's North American lands, and both wanted the large unsettled area in what is today the middle of the United States.

Between 1689 and 1763, France and England fought four wars known as the French and Indian Wars for control of North America. The French were helped by Canadians and by most of the Indians who chose one side or the other. The English were helped by the American colonists and by a lesser number of Indians. The four Colonial Wars were:

King William's War (1689-1697)
Queen Anne's War (1702-1713)
King George's War (1744-1748)
The French and Indian War (1754-1763)

Maryland took little part in the first three wars, but it was involved in the final, decisive French and Indian War. To try and win the war quickly, British lawmakers in early 1755 sent General Edward Braddock to America with 1,000 soldiers. Their first goal was to capture the French Fort

Duquesne at modern-day Pittsburgh, Pennsylvania.

Braddock assembled his men and supplies at Cumberland, Maryland, about 90 miles from Fort Duquesne. Several hundred colonial troops, including some Marylanders, joined Braddock's troops. One of the Americans, a 23-year-old Virginian named George Washington, served as an aide to General Braddock.

General Braddock and his troops on the march

The Braddock expedition left Cumberland on June 7, 1755. Because lumberjacks had to hack a trail through the woods for them, the expedition's troops, wagons, horses, and cannons moved slowly. Finally, after a month of traveling, the expedition approached Fort Duquesne on July 9, 1755. Braddock planned to attack the fort the next day, but the French, who had been warned of Braddock's approach by their Indian friends, had a deadly surprise. On July 9, several hundred French, Canadian, and Indian troops suddenly attacked Braddock's much larger army.

The capture of Fort Duquesne

Indians wait in ambush near Fort Duquesne in 1755.

The British could have won the Battle of the Wilderness, except for one thing. Like many other European generals, Braddock thought the Indians' method of shooting from behind trees and making "sneak" attacks was cowardly. The French, on the other hand, had now thrown aside the European rules of warfare and had adopted the Indian ways of fighting in the American woods. When the French forces began shooting at Braddock's troops from behind trees, George

Washington begged the general to use the same strategy. Braddock refused, and as a result the British were crushed. More than half the British troops, including some Marylanders, were killed or wounded at the Battle of the Wilderness. General Braddock himself died of wounds suffered in the battle.

As for George Washington, although two horses were shot out from under him and at least four bullets pierced his coat, he survived the battle. He also learned two lessons. The first was that the British were not unbeatable in battle as many people had thought. The second was that the key to beating them was using the Indian method, rather than fighting in an open field. These lessons served Washington well about 20 years later when the United States fought the Revolutionary War against Great Britain.

Braddock's defeat left settlements in western Maryland and Pennsylvania open to attacks by the French and the Indians. Over the next few years in these frontier regions, farms and cabins were burned, people were murdered or taken captive, and livestock were killed. Some settlers took refuge during these times in Thomas Cresap's fortified house at Oldtown, Maryland.

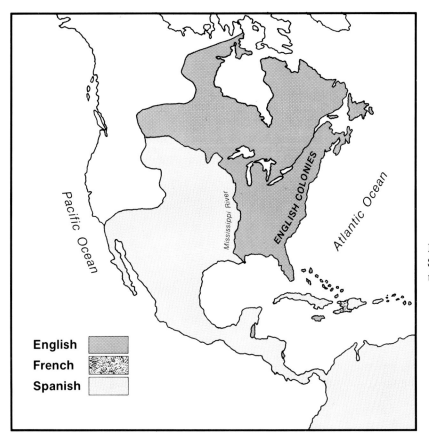

Pacific Ocean

Mississippi River

ENGLISH COLONIES

Atlantic Ocean

English	
French	
Spanish	

England, France, and Spain had colonies in the New World.

Britain finally won the French and Indian War after a long struggle in which a few hundred Marylanders took part. The pivotal clash was the Battle of Quebec, which the British won in Canada in September 1759. The war ended with the Treaty of Paris made in 1763, which gave Britain control of Canada and all French territory in the present-day United States east of the Mississippi River except New Orleans. However, England's victory in the French and Indian War set off a chain of events that ended with the mother country losing its thirteen colonies.

THOMAS CRESAP (About 1694–1790)

Thomas Cresap was born in the town of Skipton, England, but we're not sure when. One group that studied his life decided that 1694 was probably his year of birth, but at different times Cresap himself claimed to have entered the world anywhere from about 1692 to about 1704. Around the age of 15, Thomas sailed to America. Other than the fact that he settled in Maryland, the next few years of his life are just about blank for us. Then in the spring of 1727, Thomas married a young Marylander named Hannah Johnson. The couple settled in northeastern Maryland where the town of Havre de Grace (pronounced *Haverdegrass*) now stands.

The newlyweds were so poor that Thomas found himself unable to pay a small debt. Since debtors were sometimes jailed in those days, Thomas left Hannah in Maryland and went to live alone in Virginia for a time. He rented land from the family of soon-to-be-born George Washington, and there he started a farm where he hoped to live with Hannah. Two things prevented that. Thomas killed a man in a fight, and Hannah refused to leave Maryland. Thomas returned to Maryland sometime around 1728.

For a while, Cresap ran a ferryboat across the Susquehanna River in northeastern Maryland, but his mind was on the frontier. In 1729, Maryland's legislature gave him 500 acres about 50 miles up the Susquehanna from Havre de Grace near present-day Columbia, Pennsylvania. The Maryland lawmakers were happy to have Cresap move to this region that Pennsylvania also claimed. Thomas and Hannah brought a number of other people to settle this disputed area.

Cresap built a farm called Pleasant Gardens and established a ferryboat business on the Susquehanna River. From the start, Pennsylvanians claimed that the Marylanders had no right to be there. One day when Cresap was rowing two Pennsylvanians across the river, they attacked him and threw him into the water.

There were a number of skirmishes between Cresap's followers and the Pennsylvanians. Cresap even turned his home into a kind of fort and always kept a few friends nearby in case the Pennsylvanians tried to arrest him. In early 1734, Cresap or a friend shot one of a group of Pennsylvanians who tried to break into his house. The Pennsylvanians then begged Hannah Cresap for a candle so that they could look at the man's wound. Hannah refused, saying she was sorry the man had been shot in the leg—she wished "it had been his heart."

The wounded man died, and in late 1736 a 24-man Pennsylvania posse came to arrest Thomas Cresap. After an exchange of gunfire, the

Pennsylvanians burned Cresap's house. As Cresap's family and friends fled the burning home, the Pennsylvanians shot at them, wounding Thomas slightly and killing one of his friends. After his capture, the "Maryland Monster" was taken to Philadelphia, where he made his famous remark about it being one of Maryland's prettiest towns. Maryland Governor Samuel Ogle tried to have Cresap freed, but Cresap was jailed until the summer of 1737 when King George II ordered Pennsylvania and Maryland to end their border war. Thirty years later, when the Mason-Dixon line was drawn, the disputed land officially became part of Pennsylvania.

Indians had cared for Thomas Cresap's family in Maryland while he was in jail. After his release, he decided to move even farther into the wilderness. He bought many tracts of land in western Maryland. In 1741, he moved his family to a spot in far western Maryland where several Indian trails crossed. There he built a farm and trading post that were the start of Oldtown, Maryland. Cresap's house became a favorite stopping place for the Indians, who called him Big Spoon because of his generosity in feeding them and in paying for their furs. Cresap's home was also a well-known stop for colonists traveling to and from the wilderness beyond the thirteen colonies. One traveler who spent five days at Cresap's in 1748 was a 16-year-old named George Washington, who was said to have learned a great deal of woodlore from the older man.

During the rest of his long life, Cresap played a major role in helping to settle the lands west of the thirteen colonies. He helped organize the First Ohio Company in the late 1740s. A few years later, with the help of an Indian friend named Nemacolin, he built roads leading to wilderness regions. Cresap also promoted road building through western Maryland while serving as a delegate to the Maryland legislature between 1757 and 1770.

By the Revolutionary War era, Thomas Cresap was elderly even by today's standards, but that didn't stop him from working for his country's cause. In 1765, he helped organize Maryland's "Sons of Liberty," and in 1774, at about 80 years of age, he took part in the Provincial Convention that seized Maryland's government. It was said that he even wanted to fight in the Continental Army after war broke out in 1775. Although he didn't manage to do that, Thomas Cresap did live to see American independence. The "Maryland Monster," as he had once been known, died in 1790 around the age of 96.

Maryland grew rich on the export of tobacco.

Chapter VII

Life in Maryland in the 1760s

... an idea of equality also seems generally to prevail [among Marylanders] and the inferior order of people pay but little external respect to those who occupy superior stations.

William Eddis, an Englishman who came to Maryland in 1769

By 1760, when Maryland was the fourth most populous colony, its people were distributed much as they are today. Although people were scattered throughout the colony, most of them lived around Chesapeake Bay. One difference between 1760 and today is that the capital city of Annapolis was then the main Maryland town along the bay, while Frederick was the main inland town. Today, Baltimore dwarfs every other city—not only along the bay but throughout the entire state—while several of Maryland's inland cities have larger populations than Frederick.

Besides being one of the most populous colonies, Maryland was one of the most successful. King Charles I reportedly had said that Virginia was "founded upon smoke," meaning

that tobacco had made it prosperous. The same could be said of Maryland.

By the 1760s, some Marylanders had grown extremely rich by growing tobacco. Charles Carroll of Carrollton was said to be the colony's richest man. His 16-square-mile estate was worked by nearly 400 slaves. A number of other Maryland families also owned huge estates and large numbers of slaves.

The richest Marylanders lived like royalty in homes that were sometimes as big as castles. The family's "great house" was filled with the best beds, chairs, tables, grandfather clocks, and other furniture that tobacco could buy. These items, along with the family's clothes, wigs, and shoes, often came from England or Philadelphia. The family's children were taught by private tutors in little schoolhouses right on the plantation grounds. While field slaves grew the tobacco that paid for all this, house slaves dressed the plantation owners, drove them about in their carriages, and served them their meals.

Breakfast for the rich Marylanders often consisted of eggs, hot breads, biscuits, bacon, and fish or meat. The noon meal, known back then as "dinner," and the evening meal, known as "supper," often included oysters, crabs, clams, and various meats. Coffee and tea were popular with plantation families, as were such alcoholic drinks as peach brandy and persimmon beer.

Maryland's wealthiest families mingled mostly with each other and with wealthy families on the Virginia side of the Potomac River. By day, they

A colonial music lesson

did business with each other, and at night they gathered for balls at each other's homes. The rich also married one another, sometimes producing a long line of rich and famous descendants. For example, Henrietta Maria Neale of Wolleston Manor in Maryland married twice, first to the son of Virginia's governor and then to a Marylander. Among her descendants were "Light-Horse Harry" Lee of Revolutionary War fame and Robert E. Lee, commander of the Southern army during the Civil War. Another Maryland family, the Hansons, produced Declaration of Independence signer Thomas Stone as well as Presidents Benjamin Harrison and William Henry Harrison among their descendants.

The wealthy planters enjoyed many leisure activities besides balls and parties. Boat racing was popular among the wealthy men, but they didn't always race their boats themselves. When English ships arrived to buy tobacco, some

Fox hunting was a favorite pastime of the wealthy.

planters set up rowboat races between their slaves and the English crews. Crowds would gather and bet on the outcome of the race. Duck hunting and fox hunting were other popular male pastimes. Marylanders bred an excellent hunting dog, the Chesapeake Bay retriever, to fetch ducks for them, and some planters kept packs of foxhounds on their grounds for their fox-hunting outings.

The *Maryland Gazette*

Horseback riding and horse racing were passions with many rich planters, as they were with most Marylanders. An English visitor of the mid-1700s wrote that Marylanders loved riding so much "that rather than walk to church five miles, they'll go eight to catch their Horses, and ride there." Racetracks were located in several places in Maryland, the most famous being the track in Annapolis. Each September, people from throughout the South gathered in the Maryland capital to watch the Annapolis Races. George Washington spent over a week in Annapolis watching the races in late September 1771.

Printing office of the *Maryland Gazette*

George Washington attended plays as well as races while in Annapolis, since the capital was also Maryland's cultural center. The colony's first newspaper, the *Maryland Gazette*, had first been published in 1727 in Annapolis. This paper went out of business in 1734, but in 1745 it was replaced by another newspaper with the same name. Old copies of the *Gazette* reveal a great deal about the cultural life of Annapolis in the 1760s. For example, in 1760 a new theater—a remodeled warehouse—opened in Annapolis. One of the plays held that year in the Maryland capital was a tragedy called *The Orphan*. The wealthy Marylanders were the main newspaper readers and playgoers, since most other people could not read very well or afford theater tickets.

Many wealthy planters held concerts for their families and friends right in their homes. Dancing masters also toured Maryland, charging fees to teach young people the latest steps. Since photography was not yet invented, portrait painting was in demand among the wealthy. It was said that some artists traveled around with a supply of half-finished paintings showing backgrounds and people's clothes. The client would choose from these partly done paintings, and the artist would fill in the faces and hands!

It must be kept in mind that the planters' wealth came from the sweat and blood of their black slaves. By 1760, about 50,000 of Maryland's 160,000 people were slaves. The slaves—or their parents or other ancestors—had been born in Africa. The horrors of a life of slavery began along the African coast where people who had been captured by enemy tribes were locked in a kind of prison called a *barracoon*. When the white slave traders arrived, they went to the barracoon and examined the prisoners for defects. The sick and old were rejected. The young and strong were traded for such goods as metal tools and liquor. They were branded on the chest with a smoking iron so that everyone would know which slave-trading company owned them.

The slaves were then packed into a ship for the voyage to America. So that they couldn't organize a rebellion or drown themselves, the slaves were chained most of the time in a space about the size of a coffin. The crews knew that the slaves might die without fresh air and exercise, so once a day they were brought topside. Sometimes the slaves were made to dance (as best they could in their chains) and sing while the crew cracked their whips at them. Some slaves tried to die by refusing to eat. When that happened the crew would pry the slaves' mouths open and then shove the beans and rice inside.

About one-fifth of all the slaves taken to America died of disease on the ships, but they didn't have to be dead to be thrown overboard. To prevent disease from spreading throughout the ship, the

Slaves were packed on the ships for the voyage from Africa.

crews sometimes threw sick people into the ocean.

When they arrived in Maryland or another colony, the slaves were sold at auctions. Most slaves wanted to be sold to the great plantation owners such as Charles Carroll of Carrollton, rather than to the smaller farmers. The rich planters tended to buy whole families and keep them together. They felt that the slaves would be happier and would therefore work better if they were with their families. When they were sold to smaller farmers who couldn't afford many slaves, families were broken up. Sometimes the family had to be pulled apart kicking and screaming, because they knew that they would never see each other again.

Large plantations had rows of cabins that served as slave quarters, while one or two slaves might live in a barn or a hut on a small farm. The following is a former slave's description of his home on a Maryland plantation:

> We lodged in log huts, and on the bare ground. Wooden floors were an unknown luxury. In a single room were huddled, like cattle, ten or a dozen persons, men, women, and children. All ideas of refinement and decency were, of course, out of the question. There were neither bedsteads, nor furniture of any description. Our beds were collections of straw and old rags, thrown down in the corners and boxed in with boards; a single blanket the only covering. . . . The wind whistled and the rain and snow blew in through the cracks, and the damp earth soaked in the moisture till the floor was as miry as a pig-sty. Such were our houses. In these wretched hovels were we penned at night, and fed by day; here were the children born and the sick neglected.

Slaves generally worked more than 12 hours a day, every day but Sunday. Much of the slaves' work was connected with tobacco. They planted

the tobacco seeds, weeded and tended the growing plants, harvested the tobacco, and cured (dried) it. Then the slaves packed the tobacco into barrels called hogsheads, each of which typically contained 400 to 500 pounds.

The largest plantations had warehouses and landings along the riverfront. As slaves pushed from behind, oxen and horses pulled the hogsheads to the plantation warehouse. There the tobacco was stored until ships came to buy it. Many smaller farmers who lived at a distance from the riverfront had their slaves and servants clear paths to the landings. These paths, which were called "rolling roads" because the tobacco hogsheads were rolled over them, were colonial Maryland's first roadways.

The planters found plenty of work for their slaves to do in winter too. Women preserved foods and made clothes and shoes for all the people in the slave quarters for the coming year. Men chopped wood and built hogsheads.

Because their children were valuable to the planter, slave women were urged to have large families. The planter either sold the children to another planter or kept them on his property and put them to work in a few years. At about the age of five, slave children were put to work raking leaves, taking care of babies, and cleaning up the plantation grounds. By about eight, they were sent into the fields to begin their life of endless drudgery. Few slave children were taught to read or write even a little. The last thing the planters wanted was for their slaves to read the books about "liberty" and people's "natural rights" that were popular in the mid-1700s.

Young slave woman

Now and then slaves escaped, but it was difficult for them to get far. Since only 1 out of every 100 black Marylanders was a free person as of the 1760s, a lone black person often meant an escaped slave. Many people were eager to capture the escapees for the reward money. The returned slaves were usually beaten and then sent back to work.

Rich planters were at the high end of Maryland's social scale and black slaves were at the bottom. In between were the thousands of Marylanders who made up the bulk of the population. These people ranged from the smaller numbers of indentured servants who were still entering Maryland to prosperous farmers who hoped to become big planters one day.

Quite a few Maryland farmers of the 1760s lived in farmhouses made of wood or brick. In their fields they grew corn, wheat, and vegetables to feed themselves and their livestock. They also grew tobacco, which, like the big planters, they sold for things they needed. The difference was that, with a smaller tract of land and perhaps just a slave or two, the average farmer didn't make nearly as much money from tobacco as the big planter did.

Unlike the "bigwigs"—as poorer folks called the rich ones—who wore clothes from England or Philadelphia, most Marylanders wore "homespun." These were clothes made of wool or linen yarn by the women of the family. However, many people also owned a set of "Sunday" dress clothes that had cost them a lot of tobacco.

Many families, especially on Maryland's western frontier, lived much as their great-grandparents

Cutting tobacco

had. Their tables and chairs were still boards placed on logs, and their "windows" were still holes cut in the walls and covered by shutters in cold weather. Gradually, though, people were stocking their homes with store-bought goods. For example, a family might still use dried gourds for cups and whittled pieces of wood for spoons, but they might also own a few metal cups and spoons. Some families even owned a professionally made chair or two.

Even if their tobacco crop was poor, most Marylanders could still get by because they produced nearly all of their food themselves. Their eggs, bacon, and milk came from their own chickens, hogs, and cows. Corn was by far the most popular food. It was eaten in the form of

Planting corn in the backwoods

corn bread, corn stews, corn on the cob, and hominy. It was drunk in the form of corn whiskey and corn beer—often by children, too, since liquor was commonly served to the young back then.

Most of the male colonists also hunted and fished, supplying their families with venison (deer meat), oysters, crabs, fish, and terrapins. Unfortunately, the deer were thinning out in some parts of Maryland by 1760, because they had been so widely hunted for their skins. But terrapins were so numerous in early Maryland that the University of Maryland sports teams were later nicknamed the Terrapins.

Unless their family was wealthy, colonial children had a very difficult life. All day long they worked with their parents growing tobacco, sewing clothes, cooking meals, and caring for younger brothers and sisters. Few children had the opportunity to attend school. Maryland had far fewer schools than did Massachusetts and other northern colonies, partly because its farms were so scattered. No matter where a school might be built, most young people would have difficulty reaching it over the colony's poor roads. As for tutors, they were luxuries of the rich. The result was that most children learned just a little reading, writing, and arithmetic from their

This prayer book was used in the colonies.

parents—if the adults knew enough to teach them. As of 1760, about one-third of all Maryland families owned no books. Of the remaining two-thirds, most owned the Bible and perhaps one or two other books. Anyone who owned a dozen volumes was considered highly educated and a real bookworm.

Some Marylanders earned part of their living by working in business or manufacturing. The Baltimore Iron Works, founded in 1731, was Maryland's largest industrial plant, and the colony also had more than a dozen other iron-making plants. A few blacksmiths had shops where they turned the iron produced in the factories into horseshoes and farm tools. Baltimore and Annapolis also had several dozen

Blacksmith making horseshoe nails

merchant firms that bought and sold such goods as flour, grain, and tobacco. Along the coast, shipping and shipbuilding were important. But no matter what else colonial Marylanders did for a living—whether they were doctors, ministers, ironworkers, teachers, lawyers, politicians, or merchants—they almost always farmed too.

Parties, which some people called "frolics," were a favorite entertainment for many middle-class and poorer Marylanders. The country people danced jigs and reels at their frolics instead of the formal dances taught to the "bigwigs" by the dancing masters. For many families, the autumn fairs held in Baltimore and other towns were the highlight of the year. These fairs lasted four or five days and resembled the county fairs now held in many parts of the United States. Farm products were bought and sold, and there were slave raffles and horse races at these fairs.

Although they couldn't afford to run thoroughbreds in the Annapolis Races, poorer Marylanders enjoyed horse racing, too. Two farmers who disagreed about who had the faster horse would settle the question over a flat stretch of ground. Such brutal sports as boxing, cockfighting (battles to the death between two roosters), and dogfighting were also popular.

The world of politics was much different in the 1760s than it is today. In fact, if colonial Marylanders could visit the United States today they would be shocked to learn that all citizens 18 and older now have the right to vote. Women and most black people and poorer whites could not vote in colonial times. Only men who owned a certain amount of land or money could vote, and even they could only vote for certain offices, such as the House of Delegates (the lower house of the legislature). The Lord Proprietor appointed the governor as well as the Council (the upper house).

By the 1760s, thousands of Marylanders were unhappy with their political system. The complaint was often made that the government was run by Calverts, close friends of the Calverts, and men who had married Calverts. For example, in June 1769 Robert Eden, brother-in-law of Lord Proprietor Frederick Calvert, replaced longtime governor Horatio Sharpe. Many of Maryland's middle-class and poorer white males felt that it was time for them to take part in the political system too. And many people were upset about the taxes Britain had begun to impose on the colonists. Yet who could have guessed that a few years later the discontented people in Maryland and the other colonies would create a new nation?

Portraits of the men who signed
The Declaration of Independence

Chapter VIII

The Revolutionary War Era

Think, Oh! my Countrymen, to what Men become subjected when their Liberties are lost. Learn to value your own, and teach your Children to do the same, beyond Fortune or even Life.

From an article in the Maryland Gazette, *May 12, 1768*

No troops poured out their blood more freely for the common cause than those of Maryland. No troops behaved more steadily.

George Washington's praise for Maryland's Revolutionary War soldiers

From the founding of Virginia in 1607 all the way to the early 1760s, England generally left its American Colonies alone. When the Americans asked their English rulers for more say in their government, it was often granted. Laws that might have caused trouble between America and England were ignored for the most part. For example, by the early 1760s Britain had passed more than 25 Navigation Acts to make the Americans trade only with the mother country.

Thousands of Americans got around these laws by smuggling goods in and out of non-British countries. English officials knew about the smuggling, but they looked the other way. Few if any Americans saw any reason for the colonies to break free of England as of 1760. This attitude began to change after the French and Indian War ended in 1763.

The problem was that the war placed the English government in debt. To solve this problem, the English lawmakers of the 1760s decided that the colonists should pay taxes to the mother country on such items as sugar, tea, and legal papers. England also decided that it was time to enforce the Navigation Acts. Some Englishmen warned that the Americans might rebel against these laws, but they were outnumbered. The general view in England was that the Americans would gripe and groan about the taxes, but then pay them.

The Stamp Act of 1765 was one of the first of the new tax laws. Its purpose was to force Americans to buy special tax stamps and attach them to newspapers and legal papers. Nearly everyone in the thirteen colonies opposed the Stamp Act, in some cases very strongly. Massachusetts was the scene of the most violent

A protester denounces the Stamp Act

protests. In Boston, a group called the Sons of Liberty burned and smashed buildings belonging to British officials who supported the Stamp Act.

The other twelve colonies also formed Sons of Liberty and other protest groups, but they weren't as violent as the Bostonians. For example, protesters in Portsmouth, New Hampshire, carried a coffin through the streets with the words "LIBERTY—AGED 145" on it. In other colonies, crowds forced British Stamp Act officials to quit their posts or promise that they would not enforce the hated law.

After the passage of the Stamp Act in early 1765, the *Maryland Gazette* mourned the loss of

American liberty, and a young Maryland lawyer named Daniel Dulany wrote a pamphlet against the new law. Dulany presented the popular argument that "taxation without representation" is tyranny. This meant that since America was not allowed to send delegates to Britain's Parliament, Parliament had no right to tax Americans.

Threats were also made against Zachariah Hood, an Annapolis merchant who was Maryland's stamp distributor. In Annapolis and other Maryland towns, people strung up dummies that had been made to look like Hood. Rioters tore down a warehouse where he planned to store the stamps. Hood got the message. He finally fled to New York, leaving Maryland in such a hurry that he rode his horse to death.

American leaders knew that the thirteen colonies could fight the Stamp Act most effectively if they worked together. In October 1765, delegates from Maryland, Connecticut, Delaware, Massachusetts, New Jersey, New York, Pennsylvania, Rhode Island, and South Carolina attended the Stamp Act Congress in New York City. The Stamp Act Congress sent British lawmakers a message that Americans wouldn't "be taxed without their consent."

Tax stamp

The Stamp Act was supposed to take effect on November 1, 1765. That September, Governor Horatio Sharpe informed Lord Proprietor Frederick Calvert that the act could not be enforced in Maryland. His judgment was right on target. When November came, Marylanders chose to close courts and public offices rather than use the tax stamps. Georgia was the only colony where the stamps were sold, and few went into use there.

Horatio Sharpe

The Stamp Act Congress, the newspaper articles, the riots, and the Americans' refusal to use the stamps prompted the British to repeal the law in March 1766. When that news reached Maryland on May 22, 1766, both houses of the legislature adjourned to drink toasts to King George III. Things were patched up between Britain and the colonists—for a while.

The problems kept returning as England kept passing more tax laws. In 1773, the British Parliament passed the Tea Act, which Americans hated nearly as much as the Stamp Act. On December 16, 1773, about 50 Bostonians showed their feelings for the Tea Act by dumping 340 chests of British tea into Boston Harbor. This was the famous Boston Tea Party.

King George III

British lawmakers decided to punish Bostonians for the tea dumping. Among other things,

England closed Boston's port June 1, 1774, and vowed to keep it closed until the Bostonians paid for the tea they had destroyed. Even though the port closing put many of them out of work and caused a food shortage in the city, the Bostonians refused to pay for the British tea. Other colonies came to Boston's aid by sending food into the city overland. Marylanders sent corn, rye, bread, and money to Boston. People in Connecticut, New York, and Rhode Island provided corn, beef, sugar, and fish.

The Boston Tea Party inspired similar acts elsewhere. On the night of April 22, 1774, New York City patriots dumped 18 boxes of British tea into the water, and in December of that year New Jerseyans sent British tea up in smoke at the Greenwich Tea Burning. Marylanders held what was called the *Peggy Stewart* Tea Party or the *Peggy Stewart* Affair.

Anthony Stewart of Annapolis was co-owner of the *Peggy Stewart*, a ship named for his daughter. On October 15, 1774, the *Peggy Stewart* arrived in Annapolis from London carrying about a ton of British tea. People in and around Annapolis were enraged at Stewart for bringing "that detestable weed" (as the *Gazette* called it) into Maryland. Men calling themselves "Liberty Boys" debated

Burning of the *Peggy Stewart*

whether to burn Stewart's house or hang him if he didn't do something about the tea. Finally, on October 19, 1774, the terrified Anthony Stewart rowed out to the *Peggy Stewart* and burned the ship and its cargo of tea. This act convinced the Liberty Boys that Stewart was sorry he brought the tea into Maryland.

While the *Peggy Stewart* was burning in Annapolis, an important meeting was taking place in Philadelphia, Pennsylvania, about 100 miles to the northeast. Called the First Continental

Samuel Chase

William Paca

Congress (and the forerunner of the United States Congress), it was held from September 5 to October 26, 1774. Every colony but Georgia sent delegates to this meeting, which discussed ways to deal with Britain. Maryland's delegates were Samuel Chase, Robert Goldsborough, Thomas Johnson, William Paca, and Matthew Tilghman.

As was true among the general public, few delegates to the First Continental Congress wanted war with England or American independence as yet. In fact, most Americans were terrified of these ideas. They wanted only English lawmakers to grant them what they called their "rights." The First Continental Congress sent letters to Britain asking that it stop taxing Americans and punishing them for such defiant acts as the Boston Tea Party.

Yet the Americans knew that there could be a war if England didn't back down. Therefore, the First Continental Congress told the thirteen colonies to arm themselves and prepare their militias (emergency troops) for possible action. By early 1775, militia units in Maryland and other colonies were drilling for a possible war. They were soon needed, for that very spring the Revolutionary War began.

The Battle of Lexington opened the Revolutionary War.

The first shots were fired at dawn on April 19, 1775, when British troops arrived at Lexington, Massachusetts, to seize the American leaders Sam Adams and John Hancock. Adams and Hancock escaped, but Lexington militiamen faced a larger number of British troops on the Lexington village green. Eight Americans were killed and ten were wounded while just one British soldier was wounded at the Battle of Lexington.

American patriots across the Massachusetts countryside heard about the Battle of Lexington. Hundreds of them headed to nearby Concord, Massachusetts, where the British then planned to seize military supplies. Just a few hours after the Battle of Lexington, the two sides clashed again at Concord. This time the Americans outnumbered the redcoats (as British troops were nicknamed because of the color of their uniforms). The Americans pounded the redcoats at Concord's North Bridge, then chased them back toward Boston, firing at them from behind trees and walls along the way. This tactic worked for the Americans as it had for the French forces 20 years earlier in the Battle of the Wilderness. Nearly 300 redcoats were killed or wounded during the retreat to Boston. The Americans lost about 100 men in the running Battle of Concord.

Today, people around the world learn about events almost instantly, but news traveled very slowly in colonial times. Relays of horseback riders finally reached Baltimore with word of the Battles of Lexington and Concord on the evening of April 27, 1775—eight days after the clashes. Not until the morning of April 28 did the news reach Annapolis.

A confused period followed in which Marylanders and the other colonists had more questions than answers. Colonial leaders had agreed that Americans must stick together, yet many people felt that Massachusetts had brought on these battles by its warlike attitude. Would the other colonies join Massachusetts in a war against Britain, or would they decide that the war was Massachusetts' business? Had a war really begun, or were these just a couple of skirmishes that got out of hand? If a war had begun, would the colonies declare their independence from England, or would they return to British rule after fighting for their rights? Could America beat England, which was the world's strongest nation? And if the British won the war, how would they punish the Americans?

American leaders pondered these questions at the Second Continental Congress, which opened in Philadelphia on May 10, 1775, three weeks after the Lexington and Concord battles. For a while the Second Continental Congress continued to try and make peace with the mother country. Congress even sent the "Olive Branch Petition" to England asking that "harmony between [Britain] and these Colonies . . . be restored." It was written by John Dickinson, who had been born in Maryland but who represented Pennsylvania in Congress.

John Dickinson

The Battle of Bunker Hill, which was fought near Boston on June 17, 1775, proved that a major war was underway. The British won the hill they wanted, but lost about 1,000 men compared with about 400 for the Americans. Men from several other colonies fought alongside Massachussetts troops at Bunker Hill, proving that the colonists were going to stick together. Near the time of this battle, Congress began organizing the Continental Army (the forerunner of the U.S. Army). Maryland was one of the first colonies to raise troops for the army, which eventually included men from all thirteen colonies. On June 15, 1775, Congress elected Virginia's George Washington, who lived just across the Potomac River from Maryland, to command the Continental Army.

The Continental Congress told the thirteen colonies to form new governments that were free of British control. Maryland had begun doing this in 1774 by forming a temporary government called the Provincial Convention, which pushed aside the old proprietary government led by the Calverts and Governor Robert Eden. By summer of 1775, Maryland's Provincial Convention firmly controlled Maryland's government, and by the following spring some Marylanders wanted to arrest Governor Eden, who still hoped to regain the colony for the Calverts. Instead, Eden was allowed to sail out of Maryland in the summer of 1776 and return to England. After more than a

General George Washington

century as proprietors, the Calverts had lost their colony forever.

As former Governor Eden left Maryland, tension was building at the second Continental Congress in Philadelphia. On July 2, 1776, Congress was to vote on whether the thirteen colonies should declare themselves free of Great Britain. Each colony was to get one vote based on the majority vote of its delegates. On June 28, Maryland's Provincial Convention ordered its delegates to declare "the United Colonies free and independent States." When the historic vote was made on July 2, 1776, every colony but New York chose independence. New York did not vote that day, but it came out for independence a few days later.

John Trumbull painted this scene of the signing of the Declaration of Independence.

Most Continental Congressmen thought that July 2, the day they had voted for independence, would be considered the United States birthday. But on July 4, 1776, Congress adopted a paper that Virginia's Thomas Jefferson had written explaining why the United States was breaking free of England. Copies of this Declaration of Independence were sent out to the thirteen new states. Throughout the country crowds cheered, cannons were fired, and bells were rung as the Declaration of Independence was read aloud. When it was read in Baltimore in late July, people lit up the town with bonfires and threw an image of King George III into the flames.

Atop the Declaration was printed the date of its adoption—July 4, 1776. Americans loved the Declaration so much that they considered July 4—rather than July 2—to be America's Independence Day. Four men signed the Declaration of Independence for Maryland: Samuel Chase, William Paca, Thomas Stone, and Charles Carroll of Carrollton. Their signatures can be seen right below the most famous signature in American history—that of John Hancock of Massachusetts. As president of Congress, Hancock had signed the Declaration first.

In CONGRESS, July 4, 1776

The unanimous Declaration of the thirteen united States of America,

When in the Course of human events it becomes necessary for one people to dissolve the political bands which have connected them with another, and to assume among the powers of the earth, the separate and equal station to which the Laws of Nature and of Nature's God entitle them, a decent respect to the opinions of mankind requires that they should declare the causes which impel them to the separation. — We hold these truths to be self-evident, that all men are created equal, that they are endowed by their Creator with certain unalienable Rights, that among these are Life, Liberty and the pursuit of Happiness — That to secure these rights, Governments are instituted among Men, deriving their just powers from the consent of the governed, — That whenever any Form of Government becomes destructive of these ends, it is the Right of the People to alter or to abolish it, and to institute new Government, laying its foundation on such principles and organizing its powers in such form, as to them shall seem most likely to effect their Safety and Happiness. Prudence, indeed, will dictate that Governments long established should not be changed for light and transient causes; and accordingly all experience hath shewn, that mankind are more disposed to suffer, while evils are sufferable, than to right themselves by abolishing the forms to which they are accustomed. But when a long train of abuses and usurpations, pursuing invariably the same Object evinces a design to reduce them under absolute Despotism, it is their right, it is their duty, to throw off such Government, and to provide new Guards for their future security. — Such has been the patient sufferance of these Colonies; and such is now the necessity which constrains them to alter their former Systems of Government. The history of the present King of Great Britain is a history of repeated injuries and usurpations, all having in direct object the establishment of an absolute Tyranny over these States. To prove this, let Facts be submitted to a candid world.

He has refused his Assent to Laws, the most wholesome and necessary for the public good.

He has forbidden his Governors to pass Laws of immediate and pressing importance, unless suspended in their operation till his Assent should be obtained; and when so suspended, he has utterly neglected to attend to them.

He has refused to pass other Laws for the accommodation of large districts of people, unless those people would relinquish the right of Representation in the Legislature, a right inestimable to them and formidable to tyrants only.

He has called together legislative bodies at places unusual, uncomfortable, and distant from the depository of their Public Records, for the sole purpose of fatiguing them into compliance with his measures.

He has dissolved Representative Houses repeatedly, for opposing with manly firmness his invasions on the rights of the people.

He has refused for a long time, after such dissolutions, to cause others to be elected; whereby the Legislative powers, incapable of Annihilation, have returned to the People at large for their exercise; the State remaining in the mean time exposed to all the dangers of invasion from without, and convulsions within.

He has endeavoured to prevent the population of these States; for that purpose obstructing the Laws for Naturalization of Foreigners; refusing to pass others to encourage their migrations hither, and raising the conditions of new Appropriations of Lands.

He has obstructed the Administration of Justice, by refusing his Assent to Laws for establishing Judiciary powers.

He has made Judges dependent on his Will alone, for the tenure of their offices, and the amount and payment of their salaries.

He has erected a multitude of New Offices, and sent hither swarms of Officers to harrass our people, and eat out their substance.

He has kept among us, in times of peace, Standing Armies without the Consent of our legislatures.

He has affected to render the Military independent of and superior to the Civil power.

He has combined with others to subject us to a jurisdiction foreign to our constitution, and unacknowledged by our laws; giving his Assent to their Acts of pretended Legislation:

For Quartering large bodies of armed troops among us:

For protecting them, by a mock Trial, from punishment for any Murders which they should commit on the Inhabitants of these States:

For cutting off our Trade with all parts of the world:

For imposing Taxes on us without our Consent:

For depriving us in many cases, of the benefits of Trial by Jury:

For transporting us beyond Seas to be tried for pretended offences

For abolishing the free System of English Laws in a neighbouring Province, establishing therein an Arbitrary government, and enlarging its Boundaries so as to render it at once an example and fit instrument for introducing the same absolute rule into these Colonies:

For taking away our Charters, abolishing our most valuable Laws, and altering fundamentally the Forms of our Governments:

For suspending our own Legislatures, and declaring themselves invested with power to legislate for us in all cases whatsoever.

He has abdicated Government here, by declaring us out of his Protection and waging War against us.

He has plundered our seas, ravaged our Coasts, burnt our towns, and destroyed the lives of our people.

He is at this time transporting large Armies of foreign Mercenaries to compleat the works of death, desolation and tyranny, already begun with circumstances of Cruelty & perfidy scarcely paralleled in the most barbarous ages, and totally unworthy the Head of a civilized nation.

He has constrained our fellow Citizens taken Captive on the high Seas to bear Arms against their Country, to become the executioners of their friends and Brethren, or to fall themselves by their Hands.

He has excited domestic insurrections amongst us, and has endeavoured to bring on the inhabitants of our frontiers, the merciless Indian Savages, whose known rule of warfare, is an undistinguished destruction of all ages, sexes and conditions. In every stage of these Oppressions We have Petitioned for Redress in the most humble terms: Our repeated Petitions have been answered only by repeated injury. A Prince whose character is thus marked by every act which may define a Tyrant, is unfit to be the ruler of a free people.

Nor have We been wanting in attentions to our Brittish brethren. We have warned them from time to time of attempts by their legislature to extend an unwarrantable jurisdiction over us. We have reminded them of the circumstances of our emigration and settlement here. We have appealed to their native justice and magnanimity, and we have conjured them by the ties of our common kindred to disavow these usurpations, which, would inevitably interrupt our connections and correspondence. They too have been deaf to the voice of justice and of consanguinity. We must, therefore, acquiesce in the necessity, which denounces our Separation, and hold them, as we hold the rest of mankind, Enemies in War, in Peace Friends.

We, therefore, the Representatives of the united States of America, in General Congress, Assembled, appealing to the Supreme Judge of the world for the rectitude of our intentions, do, in the Name, and by Authority of the good People of these Colonies, solemnly publish and declare, That these United Colonies are, and of Right ought to be Free and Independent States; that they are Absolved from all Allegiance to the British Crown, and that all political connection between them and the State of Great Britain, is and ought to be totally dissolved; and that as Free and Independent States, they have full Power to levy War, conclude Peace, contract Alliances, establish Commerce, and to do all other Acts and Things which Independent States may of right do. — And for the support of this Declaration, with a firm reliance on the protection of Divine Providence, we mutually pledge to each other our Lives, our Fortunes and our sacred Honor.

John Hancock

Button Gwinnett
Lyman Hall
Geo Walton.

Wm Hooper
Joseph Hewes,
John Penn

Edward Rutledge.

Thos Heyward Junr.
Thomas Lynch Junr.
Arthur Middleton

Samuel Chase
Wm Paca
Thos Stone
Charles Carroll of Carrollton

George Wythe
Richard Henry Lee
Th Jefferson
Benja Harrison
Ths Nelson jr.
Francis Lightfoot Lee
Carter Braxton

Robt Morris
Benjamin Rush
Benja Franklin
John Morton
Geo Clymer
Jas Smith
Geo Taylor
James Wilson
Geo Ross
Caesar Rodney
Geo Read
Tho M:Kean

Wm Floyd
Phil. Livingston
Frans Lewis
Lewis Morris

Richd Stockton
Jno Witherspoon
Fras Hopkinson
John Hart
Abra Clark

Josiah Bartlett
Wm Whipple
Saml Adams
John Adams
Robt Treat Paine
Elbridge Gerry
Step Hopkins
William Ellery
Roger Sherman
Sam Huntington
Wm Williams
Oliver Wolcott
Matthew Thornton

The Declaration of Independence

On November 3, 1776, Maryland adopted its first state constitution (set of important laws). Instead of a House of Delegates and a Council, the state now had a House of Delegates and a Senate. The governor was elected by both houses, rather than by the people of Maryland as is done today. On February 13, 1777, Thomas Johnson was chosen as Maryland's first state governor.

To the British, the Declaration of Independence and the creation of states were just a lot of nonsense. They expected to pound the thirteen United States back into the thirteen American Colonies. During the war's first years, it often appeared that this was exactly what would happen.

The Americans were at a disadvantage in many ways. The largest American force George Washington led during the war was about 20,000 men—about half the number of the top British force. At peak strength, the American Navy had about 50 ships—about a tenth of Britain's fleet. The redcoats were also much better trained and equipped than the Americans. They had uniforms, fine weapons, food, and pay, and in turn they obeyed their officers. The U.S. government, which was still called the Continental Congress, had little money, and as a result many American soldiers fought in hunting shirts, used old guns, and were neither fed nor paid. Since their government couldn't provide properly for them, many American soldiers disobeyed their officers and even left the army when they felt like it.

Realizing that his army would be crushed in a huge battle, George Washington favored sneak attacks and smaller battles early in the war. He hoped that if he avoided losing the war long enough, his army would improve in size and discipline. He also knew that his men had the advantage of fighting on their home soil. The longer the war lasted, the more likely it was that England would grow tired of fighting a war 3,000 miles from home.

American Revolutionary War rifleman

Each of the thirteen states sent men to the Continental Army and also had its own local troops. Maryland provided about 23,000 troops in all. Although this wasn't outstanding for one of the most populous states, Maryland's soldiers gained great fame for their bravery. And although no major Revolutionary War battles were waged in Maryland, its soldiers fought in most of the big battles elsewhere.

George Washington often gave the Marylanders the most dangerous jobs, such as protecting retreating troops. For example, after the Battle of

The Battle of Long Island

Long Island, New York, in August 1776, Marylanders were assigned to cover the retreat of the defeated Continental Army. They did this so bravely that George Washington said, "No troops poured out their blood more freely for the common cause than those of Maryland." Washington's praise for Maryland's "troops of the line" at the Battle of Long Island gave Maryland its nickname—the *Old Line State.*

Marylanders also helped fight the war on the seas. Because the U.S. Navy was so small, the government hired *privateers* to attack the enemy.

Privateers were private citizens who were allowed to capture enemy ships and who received a reward for every vessel they seized. The ships in which the privateers sailed were called privateers, too. Maryland sent out about 250 of the 1,700 ships that the Continental Congress assigned as privateers. These ships aided the war effort by preventing supplies from reaching the redcoats in America. Maryland also helped the cause by producing cannons and other military supplies in its iron furnaces.

In each of the thirteen states, there were really two wars being fought. Besides the war against Britain, there was fighting between those Americans who opposed Britain and those who were loyal to the mother country. People are often suprised to learn that about a third of all Americans sided with Britain during the American Revolution. These Americans, who were called *Loyalists*, tended to be richer people who did business with Britain. Many of them actually fought on the British side, sometimes against their own relatives and neighbors.

We don't know how many Marylanders were Loyalists, but it is thought that in some parts of the Eastern Shore they were in the majority. Hundreds of men calling themselves the

"Maryland Loyalists" fought for the British army. In some areas, bands of Loyalists and patriots burned each other's crops and homes. The patriots, who controlled Maryland's government, passed laws allowing Loyalist property to be seized. As a result, many Loyalists were forced to flee Maryland or hide in the swamps of the Eastern Shore.

For several years it appeared that Britain would win the war. But gradually the American army grew in strength as George Washington had hoped. What really turned the tide, though, was France's entry into the war on America's side in February 1778. Perhaps the British would have beaten the Americans or the French alone, but they couldn't defeat the two countries fighting together.

In 1781, George Washington finally got to wage the huge battle that he had avoided for over six years. That summer, British General Charles Cornwallis led 8,000 troops into Yorktown, Virginia. Cornwallis planned to make this quiet tobacco port his headquarters for further action. Washington led his army of 17,000 Americans and Frenchmen (including about 1,100 Marylanders) toward Yorktown in late September 1781. Once at Yorktown, Washington's troops cut off the

American troops at the Battle of Yorktown

British escape by land. Meanwhile, French ships blocked the British escape by sea.

Washington's forces began firing on the British with their cannons and other heavy guns in early October 1781. They pounded the British position so fiercely that the ground began to look like the craters of the moon. By October 17, about 600 British troops had been killed or wounded in the bombardment and fighting. To save the lives of his remaining men, Cornwallis surrendered with more than 7,200 troops on October 19, 1781.

The British surrender
at Yorktown

George Washington sent Colonel Tench Tilghman, an aide from Maryland, to tell the Continental Congress in Philadelphia of the great victory at Yorktown, Virginia. The trip was 200 miles in a straight line but was really much farther because of all the winding roads and bodies of water that had to be crossed. Tilghman reached Philadelphia in just four days, in the middle of the night. He banged on the door of Thomas McKean, a Delaware man who was president of the Continental Congress, to tell him the great news.

The national lawmakers in Philadelphia and American patriots everywhere celebrated the victory at Yorktown. In many towns in Maryland and the other states, people drank thirteen toasts and fired thirteen-round cannon salutes to the thirteen United States. The British and the American Loyalists, on the other hand, mourned the outcome of the Battle of Yorktown. When the news reached London, England, British Prime Minister Lord Frederick North said, "Oh God, it is all over." Although the peace treaty acknowledging the American victory wasn't signed until 1783, the Battle of Yorktown marked the end of major Revolutionary War fighting.

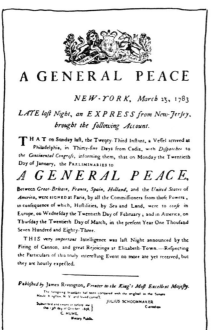

A broadside distributed in New York City announces the end of the Revolutionary War.

CHARLES CARROLL OF CARROLLTON (1737–1832)

Charles Carroll of Carrollton

In 1688, Charles Carroll the attorney general (as he is known) moved from Ireland to Maryland, where he hoped to practice his Catholic religion in peace. He accumulated 60,000 acres of land and served briefly as Maryland's attorney general. When Protestants seized Maryland in 1689, Charles Carroll the attorney general remained loyal to Lord Baltimore, and was jailed several times for insulting the people who took over the colony.

One of the attorney general's sons, Charles Carroll of Annapolis, became one of the richest men in America and was also a rebel like his father. He fought with Maryland's governors over the fact that Catholics could no longer vote, have their own schools, practice law, or hold public office in the colony. Charles Carroll of Annapolis and his wife had one son, who was called Charles Carroll of Carrollton for an estate the family owned in Frederick County, Maryland.

Although they were outlawed, a few Catholic schools were secretly run by priests in private Maryland homes. Charles Carroll of Carrollton attended one of these schools. At the age of 10, he was sent to Europe to complete his education. While studying Greek, Latin, and literature, young Charles was not told about the mistreatment of Maryland's Catholics. Perhaps because Charles was their only child and was small and sickly, his parents wanted to protect him.

In 1757, Charles's father visited him in Paris and told him about what was happening to the Catholics in Maryland. Twenty-year-old Charles was shocked. He was also upset to learn that his father wanted him to study law. He argued that this wouldn't do him any good, since Catholics couldn't work as lawyers in Maryland. But his father felt that knowledge of law would help him protect and increase the family fortune. Although he hated it, Charles studied law in Europe for the next few years. Finally, in early 1765 he returned to the Maryland home that he hadn't seen for 18 years.

Soon after his return, Britain's Parliament passed the Stamp Act. As one of America's richest men (some people claimed he was *the* richest), Charles Carroll of Carrollton might have been expected to side with England like most other wealthy people. However, he hated England for oppressing Catholics in both Ireland and America for so long. He risked not only his fortune but his life in support of America's cause.

In 1773, Carroll began writing anti-British articles for the *Maryland Gazette* and the next year he took part in the *Peggy Stewart* Tea Party. Then in early 1776, the Continental Congress appointed him to head north and try to persuade the Canadians to fight on America's side.

Benjamin Franklin of Pennsylvania and Carroll's fellow Marylanders Samuel Chase and Father John Carroll accompanied him. Father Carroll (his cousin) later became the first Catholic bishop in the United States and also founded Georgetown University in present-day Washington, D.C.

On July 4, 1776, just a few days after returning home from this fruitless mission, Charles Carroll of Carrollton was elected to represent Maryland at the Continental Congress. It was too late for him to vote for independence, but since most of the delegates didn't place their names on the Declaration until about two months later, he took part in the signing. He was the only Catholic signer.

During the next quarter century, Charles Carroll of Carrollton served his state and country in many ways. He helped write Maryland's first state constitution in 1776, was a member of Maryland's first state senate, and served as one of its first two U.S. senators.

Charles Carroll of Carrollton retired from politics in 1801, but he remained active long after that. Even in his eighties he rode his horse 20 miles in the morning to oversee his lands and visit with neighbors. Despite the fact that he was Maryland's largest slaveholder, he seems to have turned against slavery later in life. From time to time, he freed some of his slaves, including 30 of them at once in 1817 when he was 80 years old. He was also on the first board of directors of the Baltimore and Ohio Railroad, the first railroad in the Americas to carry both people and freight. He laid the cornerstone for this famous railroad in 1828 at the age of 91.

For the last few years of his life, Charles Carroll of Carrollton was the only living signer of the Declaration of Independence. People who didn't even know him would come by just to stare at him or shake his hand. He died at his home in Baltimore at the age of 95.

The Maryland State House in Annapolis. It was here that Congress
ratified the Treaty of Paris that ended the Revolutionary War.

Chapter IX

The Seventh State

Comparing . . . the evils which we labor under and may experience from the present confederation [the United States government under the Articles of Confederation] . . . I am clear that I ought to give it [the new United States Constitution] all the support in my power.

> *From James McHenry's notebook entry of September 17, 1787, the day he signed the United States Constitution*

On September 3, 1783, American and British representatives in Paris, France, signed the treaty ending the Revolutionary War. England's recognition of America's independence did not mean the end of the new nation's troubles, though. During the 1780s it appeared that England or some other country could take over the United States just by waiting a few years. The United States seemed to be collapsing from within for two main reasons. The central government was too weak, and the thirteen states were always arguing.

A set of laws called the Articles of Confederation provided for the nation's government. When first written by John Dickinson in 1776, the Articles provided for a rather strong central government. Too strong, the congressmen felt, and refused to approve the Articles at that point. Southerners feared that Northerners would gain the upper hand in a strong central government and vice versa. Small states feared that big states would become too powerful and vice versa. And everyone was afraid that a powerful central government would do what the British had attempted—TAX THEM! As a result, Congress kept watering down the Articles. By the time Congress adopted the Articles of Confederation in November 1777 they created a U.S. government that in many ways was weaker than each of the state governments!

The Articles weren't to take effect until ratified (approved) by all thirteen states. By late February 1779, every state but Maryland had ratified the Articles. Maryland objected to the claim by Virginia and a few other states to the "western lands" beyond the thirteen states. Maryland argued that the western lands should be held by the central government for the good of the whole nation, instead of benefiting just a few states. Maryland wouldn't approve the Articles until this was done, causing a feud between the Old Line State and Virginia. Finally, the states claiming the western lands gave in, and Maryland approved the Articles on March 1, 1781, 3½ years after they had been adopted by Congress.

Under the Articles of Confederation, the national government lacked many powers that we now take for granted. True, there were no national taxes, but at what a price! The country had no national courts, no president to lead it, no national money (each state made its own), no permanent national capital, and just a tiny U.S. Army. The national government, which was officially called the Congress of the Confederation but which people still called the Continental Congress, didn't always attract the best law-makers. The best people often chose to serve in state government, which was considered more important than the national government.

Several events proved that the government under the Articles was too weak. One of them had a Maryland connection. Between 1774 and 1800, when Washington, D.C., became the nation's permanent capital, eight different cities served as the seat of government. Had the Declaration of Independence been issued a few months later it would have been signed in Baltimore, which was

Annapolis, Maryland was the nation's capital for seven months.

the U.S. capital from December 20, 1776, to March 4, 1777. Annapolis was the nation's capital from November 26, 1783, to June 3, 1784. As soon as the lawmakers began meeting in Annapolis, they faced a problem concerning the peace treaty that had been signed in Paris, France, in September 1783. The treaty wouldn't become official unless it was signed by Congress and returned to Paris by March 3, 1784.

The treaty favored the United States, so its contents posed no difficulty. The problem was that at least nine states had to approve the treaty according to the Articles of Confederation. By the end of 1783, only seven states were sufficiently represented in Annapolis to approve the treaty. As often happened, several states hadn't sent delegates to Congress! The treaty wasn't approved by Congress until February 14, 1784. Since ships took several weeks to cross the ocean, the signed treaty didn't reach Paris until a month past deadline. Fortunately, England didn't use this tardiness as an excuse to back out of the peace agreement.

Another event that pointed up the central government's lack of muscle was Shays' Rebellion, which lasted from September 1786 to February 1787. Led by Daniel Shays, this was a revolt by western Massachusetts farmers who opposed high state taxes and laws that jailed debtors. The U.S. Army, which then had only about 700 men, couldn't put down Shays' Rebellion, so the Massachusetts militia had to do it. People realized that unless the U.S. government was strengthened, the whole country might be toppled by some future rebellion.

A mob in
possession of
a courthouse
during Shays'
Rebellion

In September 1786—when Shays' Rebellion began—the seeds for a stronger government were sown at the Annapolis Convention. This conference was held in the Maryland capital to discuss ways of handling certain disputes between states. Although Maryland hosted the meeting, Virginia planned it and issued the invitations to all thirteen states. Only Delaware, New Jersey, New York, Pennsylvania, and Virginia showed up. Maryland and the other seven states felt that such a meeting should have Congress's blessing.

Daniel Shays

Although the Annapolis Convention didn't accomplish much, its delegates suggested that a larger meeting be held in Philadelphia. Congress would organize this meeting, which would revise the Articles of Confederation.

Only Rhode Island refused Congress's invitation to attend the convention that opened in Philadelphia in May 1787. Maryland's five delegates were James McHenry, Daniel Carroll (a cousin of Charles Carroll of Carrollton), Daniel of St. Thomas Jenifer, Luther Martin, and John F. Mercer. The convention went far beyond its assignment. Instead of revising the Articles, it created a whole new set of national laws—the United States Constitution. Luther Martin and

Luther Martin

John F. Mercer were shocked at the great power the new Constitution gave the central government, and would not sign the paper. McHenry, Carroll, and Jenifer signed the Constitution for the Old Line State.

Each of the thirteen states would join the United States under its new Constitution the moment it approved the paper. Delaware approved the Constitution first on December 7, 1787, earning the nickname the *First State*. A Maryland state convention held in Annapolis approved the Constitution on April 28, 1788. With that vote, Maryland—which had been the home of Nanticoke Indians, Margaret Brent, and Thomas Cresap, and which had provided two early United States capitals and would soon provide land for Washington, D.C.—became the seventh state!

BENJAMIN BANNEKER (1731-1806)

One day about 1680 a young servant in England named Molly Welsh was arrested for stealing a pail of milk that had really been kicked over by a cow. In England at that time, stealing could be punished by death, but like many other people Molly was spared by agreeing to go to America as an indentured servant. She reached Maryland around 1683, and worked for a tobacco planter on the Patapsco River near present-day Baltimore for about seven years.

After her release, Molly Welsh started her own farm in the same area. Her farm did so well that in 1692 she bought two black slaves to help with the work. Several years later, Molly freed both slaves and then did something very unusual for a colonial white woman. She married one of the former slaves, whose name was Banneky. More than 30 years later, Molly and Banneky's daughter, Mary, also married a freed slave, whose name was Robert. Since Robert had no last name of his own, he and Mary used Mary's last name—Banneky. The first of Mary and Robert Banneky's four children was a son named Benjamin. Later his last name was changed slightly so that he became Benjamin Banneker.

Benjamin Banneker

At first Benjamin and his family lived on the farm of Grandmother Molly Welsh. Even after his parents bought a nearby farm, Benjamin continued to spend a great deal of time with his grandmother, who taught him to read and write. Seeing that Benjamin was very bright, Molly Welsh sent him to a nearby one-room school. Many years later, a classmate said that Benjamin hadn't enjoyed children's games in his youth, but that "all his delight was to dive into his books." Although Benjamin wasn't able to attend school for very long, he borrowed books whenever possible and read them after a day of working with his father in their tobacco fields and cornfields.

When Benjamin was about 20, someone lent the serious and quiet young man a pocket watch and let him take it apart. Based on what he saw, Benjamin built a wooden clock in 1753. This would have been an achievement for anyone, but people were especially impressed because Benjamin was black. There was a widespread belief among the white colonists that black people were not intelligent and were therefore "meant for slavery." Benjamin's clock, which kept nearly perfect time for half a century, proved that blacks could achieve a great deal if given the chance. People came from miles around to see the clock made by 22-year-old Benjamin Banneker.

Until rather late in life, Benjamin had little opportunity to put his mathematical and scientific interests to use. When Benjamin was 28 his father died, leaving him to run the farm and care for his mother and sisters. Benjamin couldn't even afford to buy his first book—the Bible—until he was 31 years old.

The turning point in Benjamin's life occurred in 1773 when the Ellicott family moved near his home. The Ellicotts built a store and also mills for sawing wood and grinding grain. A town called Ellicott City (just west of Baltimore) grew up at this settlement. Banneker began spending time at the store where he read newspapers and became friendly with several of the Ellicotts. George Ellicott, who was 29 years younger than Benjamin, lent him a telescope and astronomy books. From then on, Benjamin spent clear nights studying the stars with the telescope.

In 1791 it was decided that a new permanent U.S. capital would be carved out of a piece of Maryland. Andrew Ellicott was hired to survey (determine the boundaries of) the new capital—Washington, D.C. In those days, a great deal of astronomy was involved in surveying. Because Banneker was a fine astronomer and a family friend, Andrew Ellicott hired him for his surveying team. Banneker accompanied Ellicott to the site of the new capital. By night, Benjamin made his astronomical observations, then slept in a tent during the day. Sixty-year-old Benjamin Banneker spent about three months of early 1791 helping to lay out Washington, D.C., before returning home that spring.

Shortly afterward, Benjamin Banneker began publishing *Benjamin Banneker's Almanac.* This book told when the sun and moon would rise and set for the coming year, predicted the weather, and contained witty sayings and poems like Benjamin Franklin's more famous *Poor Richard's Almanac. Banneker's Almanac*, which became very popular, was published for about six years in the 1790s.

Like the clock he made nearly half a century earlier, Banneker's almanacs convinced many people that blacks could accomplish as much as whites if given the opportunity. Benjamin Banneker, who never married, spent his last years observing the stars and playing his violin and flute. He died just before his 75th birthday in his log home near Baltimore.

CHARLES WILLSON PEALE (1741-1827)

Charles Willson Peale was born in Queen Annes County on Maryland's Eastern Shore. His father was an Englishman who had been banished to America a few years earlier for stealing money from his employer. In Maryland, Mr. Peale became a schoolteacher. He taught in several Maryland schools, including King William's School in Annapolis.

Charles's father taught him reading, writing, and Latin in the hope that he would go to college. But when Charles was nine years old his father died, leaving the family poor. When Charles was not quite 13, his mother apprenticed him to an Annapolis saddle maker. The agreement was that Charles would work for the saddle maker, almost like an indentured servant, until he reached the age of 21.

For the next eight years, Charles spent his days making saddles. Now and then he drew a picture or took a watch apart, but by the age of 20 he had not yet shown the artistic or scientific talent that would later make him famous. In early 1762, when he was not quite 21, Charles was released from his apprenticeship and married a 17-year-old Marylander named Rachel Brewer. Charles then opened his own saddle shop in Annapolis.

Charles Willson Peale

Charles had been in business for just a short time when he made a trip to Norfolk, Virginia, to buy leather. He saw some paintings in Norfolk that inspired him—not because they were so good but because he felt he could do better. Charles painted a few portraits of friends and family, and soon decided to become a professional artist. He wasn't very good at first, though, and for a time most of his artistic work consisted of painting signs.

Peale knew that he could only succeed if he learned more, so around 1763 he went to Philadelphia where he met artists and bought a book on art. Around this time he also became friendly with John Hesselius, a well-known artist who lived near Annapolis. In exchange for a saddle, Hesselius gave him painting lessons. Hesselius would paint half a face, then Peale would finish the portrait. Peale improved so rapidly that some prominent Marylanders including Governor Horatio Sharpe and Charles Carroll of Carrollton sent him to study art in England for about two years. By the time Peale returned to Annapolis in the summer of 1769 most people who saw his work considered him one of the best artists in the thirteen colonies.

Until nearly the end of his long life, Charles Willson Peale painted portraits of some of the most famous Americans. In 1772 he went to Mount Vernon in Virginia where he painted the first known portrait of George Washington. In all, he painted nearly 60 portraits of Washington as well as portraits of Presidents Thomas Jefferson, James Monroe, and John Quincy Adams.

At the start of the Revolution, Peale moved with his family to Philadelphia, Pennsylvania. Despite his gentle nature, he was a firm patriot, and even fought with the Continental Army at Trenton and Princeton, New Jersey. The stress of the war—especially the fighting between the patriots and the Loyalists—resulted in a mental breakdown for Peale. During the last two years of the war, he suffered from a partial loss of memory and didn't return to normal until the peace treaty was signed.

Despite his fame, Peale had trouble earning a living from his art. All his life, he did other jobs to help support his large family. Besides painting a man's portrait he might make him false teeth and glasses and also fix his watch! But his main life's work besides art was the "Peale Museum," which he founded during the 1780s in his Philadelphia home. The museum, which later moved to larger quarters in Philadelphia, displayed rocks and minerals, stuffed animals, and skeletons of such creatures as the prehistoric mastodon. In the 1780s Peale built a little theater in his museum where he showed what he called "moving pictures." These were pictures on a clear surface which he lit from behind and changed to give the feeling of motion. Peale's "moving pictures" were a forerunner of the modern-day movies that were invented about a century later.

Charles Willson Peale, who outlived Rachel and two other wives, was the father of seventeen children. He named many of his children for great artists in the hope that they would become artists too, and he taught them all he knew about painting. Among the children named for artists were Raphaelle, Rembrandt, Rubens, and two sons (the first died young) named Titian Peale. As if he didn't have enough children, for a while Peale turned his museum into a kind of day-care center for lost and neglected children. Making life even more interesting for the Peale family were the rattlesnakes, monkeys, and bears that were always arriving at their door for display in the museum.

Charles Willson Peale believed that people could live to 112 by eating healthy foods and avoiding liquor. At the age of 80, he was still riding around the Philadelphia area on a kind of early bicycle called a velocipede. He was working on convincing a woman (for whom he had made a set of false teeth) to become his fourth wife when he became ill and died at the age of 85. His sons Raphaelle and Rembrandt Peale became famous artists as he had hoped. In 1814, Rembrandt Peale founded the Peale Museum in Baltimore, which today is one of the oldest American museums. Charles Willson Peale's niece, Sarah Miriam Peale, was one of the first women to become a portrait artist in the United States.

JAMES McHENRY (1753-1816)

By the mid-1500s, the Roman Catholic nation of Ireland had been conquered by England, its powerful neighbor to the east. The English, who were Protestants, outlawed Catholic worship in Ireland and murdered priests. They also pushed many Irish-Catholics off their lands and replaced them with Protestants from Scotland. The Scottish people who were transplanted to Ireland became known as the Scotch-Irish.

James McHenry was born into a Scotch-Irish family not far from Belfast in what is now Northern Ireland. His father, a well-to-do merchant, sent him to a fine school in Dublin, Ireland. When James was about 17, his health broke down. For reasons that are unclear, he decided to go to America. He arrived in Philadelphia in 1771 and liked it so much that he soon convinced his parents and younger brother to join him in the new country. Shortly after arriving in Philadelphia, James McHenry met a 9-year-old girl named Peggy Caldwell whom he taught to write the alphabet. A few years later Peggy would become a very important part of his life.

James McHenry

James decided that he wanted to become a doctor. In those days, most American men who wanted to become doctors (there were no female physicians yet) studied with other doctors rather than in medical schools. McHenry studied medicine in Philadelphia under the famous Dr. Benjamin Rush. Sometime around James McHenry's 21st birthday, Rush decided that James was qualified, and from then on he was Dr. McHenry.

Not long after that, the Revolutionary War began. Most Americans of Irish and Scotch-Irish background opposed England in the war. The Irish hated England for trying to destroy Catholicism and their way of life in Ireland. Many Scotch-Irish people disliked England for discriminating against them in Ireland. Dr. McHenry sided with his new country more firmly than most people who had lived in America all their lives.

Within weeks of the outbreak of the war, McHenry hurried to Cambridge, Massachusetts, where he worked as a volunteer in American hospitals. By the summer of 1776 he was working as a surgeon for the American army in the New York City region, which the British were about to seize from the patriots. On November 16, 1776, James McHenry was captured along with about 3,000 other Americans at Fort Washington in what is now New York City. During his captivity, he was allowed to treat other American prisoners who were wounded or sick. The British paroled him in early 1777.

McHenry worked as a doctor in the Continental Army a while longer, but then in May 1778 George Washington appointed him as his secretary. With this appointment, McHenry gave up medicine and spent the rest of his working life involved with military affairs and politics. George Washington, who didn't make friends easily, grew to love McHenry for his loyalty and devotion to the cause. In August 1780, General Washington assigned McHenry to assist the Marquis de Lafayette, a young French officer who had come to help the Americans fight England. McHenry was the Frenchman's aide until after the Battle of Yorktown.

Now and then James McHenry had spent time in Baltimore, where his father and brother had established a business before the war. While away at the Battle of Yorktown in the fall of 1781, McHenry was elected to the Maryland Senate. Over the next years "Mac" (as his friends called him) served in both the state senate and as a Maryland delegate to the Continental Congress. A happy event in his personal life took place in 1784 when he married Peggy Caldwell, the girl who had learned the alphabet from him a few years earlier. The couple settled in the Baltimore area and had five children.

In the spring of 1787, McHenry was elected to represent Maryland at the Constitutional Convention in Philadelphia, where he worked quietly to help create the new national laws. Although McHenry disliked some parts of the new Constitution, he knew that it was much better than the Articles of Confederation. He signed the Constitution and helped convince the Maryland convention that met in Annapolis to approve it on April 28, 1788.

James McHenry remained in Maryland politics for the next few years. Then in early 1796 his old friend George Washington made him United States secretary of war—a post he held until 1800. McHenry then retired to Baltimore, where he lived until his death in 1816 at the age of 62. This quiet man who had served his country as a doctor, aide to Washington and Lafayette, and secretary of war, had one more claim to fame. Baltimore's Fort McHenry, where the flag flew that inspired Francis Scott Key to write "The Star-Spangled Banner" in 1814, was named for him.

In recognition of his service to the Crown, especially in the capacity of the King's Principal Secretary, Sir George Calvert was granted the title of Baron Baltimore of Baltimore in Ireland. A miniature portrait of James I of England is at the upper left.

Maryland

This Province was so called by King Charles I, in honour of his beloved Queen Henrietta Maria, when he gave it by Charter to Calvert Lord Baltimore, in whose Family the Property still continues. But the Nomination of the Governor & Council has been in the Crown ever since y Reign of King William. As y first Lords Proprietors were Roman Catholicks, the Original Planters were chiefly of that Religion: But those of the Church of England are now more numerous than the Papists and Dissenters together. They are in the whole computed at about Thirty Thousand.

Maryland lies on both sides of y Bay of Chesapeak, and is bounded on the South by Virginia, on the East by the Atlantic Ocean, on the North by Pensylvania, and on y West by the Apalachean Mountains. The chief Rivers are Patowmack,

Document describing the Maryland Colony is in the archives of the
Maryland Historical Society in Baltimore, Maryland.

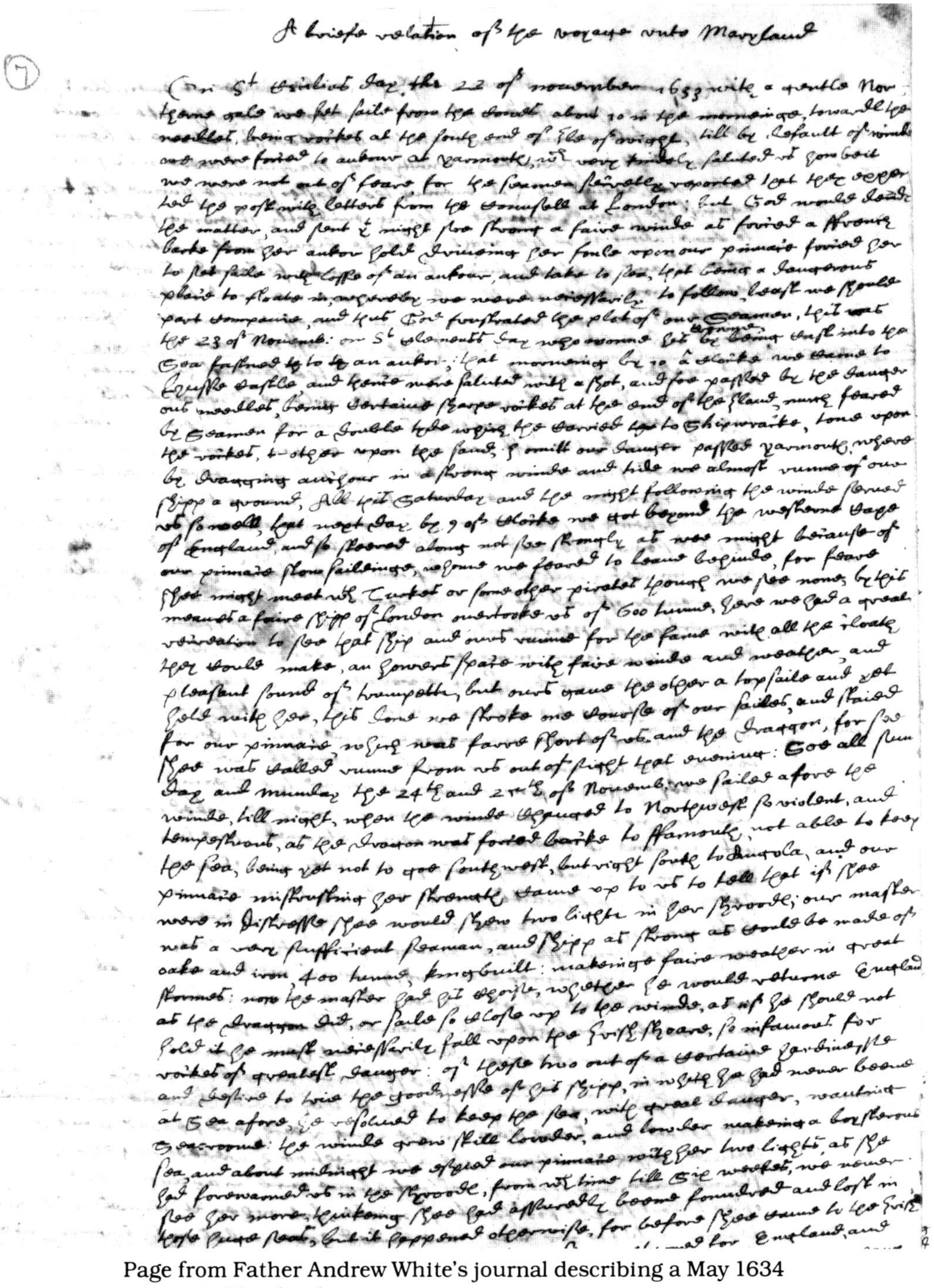
A briefe relation of the voyage unto Maryland

Page from Father Andrew White's journal describing a May 1634 voyage to Maryland.

MARYLAND CALVERT PAPERS. HISTORICAL SOCIETY

At the Castle at Windsor Easter Tuesday 1765 Rec.ᵈ then of the R.ᵗ Hon.ᵇᵉ Frederick Lord Baron of Baltimore of Ireland, Lord and Proprietor of the Province of Maryland in America, rec.ᵈ two Indian Arrows of the said province from the Hon.ᵇᵉ Cæcilius Calvert the provincial Sec.ʸ Rec.ᵈ as an Annual Rent due to His Majesty as Tenure Rent his Lord.ˢ Tenure for the said province, payable by his Royal Charter this Day at His Majesty's Castle at Windsor.

Rec.ᵈ for the use of His Majesty.

Rec.ᵈ April the 9. 1765 of the Hon.ᵇᵉ M.ʳ Calvert two Indian arrows in the absence of the Hon.ᵇᵉ General Brudenell deputy Governor of Windsor Castle & Will.ᵐ Jarman Gunner

The first year's rent for the province of Maryland—two Indian arrows—was paid by Cecil Calvert, Second Lord Baltimore, to the Deputy Constable of Windsor Castle on April 23, 1633.

A LAW
OF
MARYLAND
Concerning
RELIGION.

 Oraſ nuch as in awell-governed and Chriſtian Commonwealth, Matters concerning Religion and the Honour of God ought to be in the firſt pla e to be taken into ſerious conſideration, and endeavoured to be ſettled. Be it therefore Ordained and Enacted by the Right Honourable CÆCILIUS Lord Baron of Baltemore, abſolute Lord and Proprietary of this Province, with the Advice and Conſent of the Upper and Lower Houſe of this General Aſſembly, That whatſoever perſon or perſons within this Province and the Iſlands thereunto belonging, ſhall fro.n henceforth blaſpheme GOD, that is curſe him; or ſhall deny our Saviour JESUS CHRIST to be the Son of God; or ſhall deny the Holy Trinity, the Father, Son, & Holy Ghoſt; or the Godhead of any of the ſaidThreePerſons of the Trinity, or the Unity of theGodhead, or ſhall uſe or utter any reproachful ſpeeches, words, or language, concerning the Holy Trinity, or any of the ſaid three Perſons thereof, ſhall be puniſhed with death, and confiſcation or forfeiture of all his or her Lands and Goods to the Lord Proprietary and his Heirs.

And be it alſo enacted by the Authority, and with the advice and aſſent aforeſaid, That whatſoever perſon or perſons ſhall from henceforth uſe or utter any reproachful words or ſpeeches concerning the bleſſed Virgin MARY, the Mother of our Saviour, or the holy Apoſtles or Evangeliſts, or any of them, ſhall in ſuch caſe for the firſt Offence forfeit to the ſaid Lord Proprietary and his Heirs, Lords and Proprietaries of this Province, the ſum of Five pounds Sterling, or the value thereof to be levied on the goods and chattels of every ſuch perſon ſo offending; but in caſe ſuch offender or offenders ſhall not then have goods and chattels ſufficient for the ſatisfying of ſuch forfeiture, or that the ſame be not otherwiſe ſpeedily ſatisfied, that then ſuch offender or offenders ſhall be publickly whipt, and be impriſoned during the pleaſure of the Lord Proprietary, or the Lieutenant or Chief Governor of this Province for the time being: And that every ſuch offender and offenders for every ſecond offence ſhall forfeit Ten Pounds Sterling, or the value thereof to be levied as aforeſaid; or in caſe ſuch offender or offenders ſhall not then have goods and chattels within this Province ſufficient for that purpoſe, then to be publickly and ſeverely whipt and impriſoned as before is expreſſed : and that every perſon or perſons before mentioned, offending herein the third time, ſhall for ſuch third offence, forfeit all his lands and goods, and be for ever baniſht and expelled out of this Province.

And be it alſo further Enacted by the ſame Authority, advice and aſſent, That whatſoever perſon or perſons ſhall from henceforth upon any occaſion of offence, or otherwiſe in a reproachful manner or way, declare, call, or denominate, any perſon or perſons whatſoever, inhabiting, reſiding, trafficking, trading, or commercing within thisProvince, or within any the Ports, Harbours, Creeks orHavens to the ſame belonging, an Heretick, Schiſmatick, Idolater, Puritan, Presbyterian, Independant, PopiſhPrieſt, Jeſuit, JeſuitedPapiſt, Lutheran, Calviniſt, Anabaptiſt, Browniſt, Antinomian, Roundhead, Separatiſt, or other name or term in a reprcachfull manner relating to matter of Religion, ſhall for every ſuch offence forfeit and loſe the ſum of Ten ſhillings Sterling, or the value thereof, to be levied of the goods and chattels of every ſuch offender and offenders, the one half thereof to be forfeited and paid unto the perſon & perſons of whom ſuch reproachful words are, or ſhall be ſpoken or uttered, and the other half thereof to the Lord Proprietary and his Heirs, Lords and Proprietaries of this Province : But if ſuch perſon or perſons who ſhall at any time uttter or ſpeak any ſuch reproachful words or language, ſhall not have goods or chattels ſufficient and overt within this Province to be taken to ſatisfy the penalty aforeſaid, or that the ſame be not otherwiſe ſpeedily ſatisfied, that then the perſon and perſons ſo offending ſhall be publickly whipt, and ſhall ſuffer impriſonment without Bail or Mainpriſe untill he, ſhe, or they, reſpectively, ſhall ſatisfie the party offended or grieved by ſuch reproachfull Language, by asking him or her reſpectively forgiveneſs publickly, for ſuch his offence, before the Magiſtrate or chief Officer or Officers of the Town or place where ſuch offence ſhall be given.

And be it further likewiſe enacted by the authority and conſent aforeſaid, that every perſon and perſons within this Province, that ſhall at any time hereafter prophane the Sabbath, or Lords day, called Sunday, by frequent ſwearing, drunkenneſs, or by any uncivil or diſorderly Recreation, or by working on that day when abſolute neceſſity doth not require, ſhall for every ſuch firſt offence forfeit two ſhillings ſix pence Sterling, or the value thereof; and for the ſecond offence five ſhillings Sterling, or the value thereof; and for the third offence, and for every time he ſhall offend in like manner afterwards, Ten ſhillings Sterling, or the value thereof; and in caſe ſuch offender or offenders ſhall not have ſufficient goods or chattels within this Province to ſatisfy any of the aforeſaid penalties reſpectively hereby impoſed for prophaning the Sabbath or Lords day called Sunday as aforeſaid, then in every ſuch caſe the party ſo offending ſhall for the firſt and ſecond offence in that kind be impriſoned till he or ſhe ſhall publickly in open Court before the chief Commander, Judge or Magiſtrate of that County, Town, or Precinct wherein ſuch offence ſhall be committed, acknowledge the ſcandal and offence he hath in that reſpect given, againſt God, and the good and civil Government of this Province: and for the third offence and for every time after ſhall alſo be publickly whipt.

And whereas the inforcing of the Conſcience in matter of Religion hath frequently fallen out to be of dangerous conſequence in thoſe Commonwealths where it hath been practiſed, and for the more quiet and peaceable Government of this Province, and the better to preſerve mutual love & unity amongſt the Inhabitants here, Be it therefore alſo by the Lord Proprietary with the advice and aſſent of this Aſſembly, ordained and enacted, except as in this preſent Act is before declared and ſet forth, that no perſon or perſons whatſoever within this Province, or the Iſlands, Ports, Harbors, Creeks, or Havens thereunto belonging, profeſſing to believe in Jeſus Chriſt, ſhall from henceforth be any ways troubled, moleſted, or diſcountenanced, for, or in reſpect of his or her Religion nor in the free exerciſe thereof within this Province or the Iſlands thereunto belonging, nor any way compell'd to the belief or exerciſe of any otherReligion, againſt his or her conſent, ſo as they be not unfaithfull to the Lord Proprietary, or moleſt or conſpire againſt the civil Government, eſtabliſhed or to be eſtabliſhed in this Province under him and his Heirs. And that all and every perſon and perſons that ſhall preſume contrary to this Act and the true intent & meaning thereof, directly or indirectly, either in perſon or eſtate, wilfully to wrong, diſturb, or trouble, or moleſt, any perſon or perſons whatſoever within this Province, profeſſing to believe in Jeſus Chriſt, for or in reſpect of his or herReligion, or the free exerciſe thereof within thisProvince, otherwiſe then is provided for in this Act, that ſuch perſon or perſons ſo offending ſhall be compelled to pay treble damages to the party ſo wronged or moleſted, and for every ſuch offence ſhall alſo forfeit Twenty ſhillings Sterling in Money, or the value thereof, half thereof for the uſe of the LordProprietary and his Heirs, Lords and Proprietaries of this Province, and the other half thereof for the uſe of the Party ſo wronged or moleſted as aforeſaid; or if the party ſo offending as aforeſaid, ſhall refuſe or be unable to recompence the party ſo wronged, or to ſatisfy ſuch fine orforfeiture, then ſuch offender ſhall be ſeverely puniſhed by publick whipping and impriſonment during the pleaſure of the Lord Proprietary or his Lieutenant or chief Governor of this Province for the time being, without Bail or Mainpriſe.

And be it further alſo enacted by the authority and conſent aforeſaid, that the Sheriff or other Officer or Officers from time to time to be appointed and authorized for that purpoſe of the County, Town, or Precinct where every particular offence in this preſent Act contained, ſhall happen at any time to be committed, and whereupon there is hereby a forfeiture, fine, or penalty impoſed, ſhall from time to time diſtrain, and ſeize the goods and eſtate of every ſuch perſon ſo offending as aforeſaid againſt this preſent Act or any part thereof, and ſell the ſame or any part thereof for the full ſatisfaction of ſuch forfeiture, fine, or penalty as aforeſaid, reſtoring to the party ſo offending, the remainder or over plus of the ſaid goods or eſtate, after ſuch ſatisfaction ſo made as aforeſaid.

Copy of the Toleration Act

Colonial America Time Line

Before the arrival of Europeans, many millions of Indians belonging to dozens of tribes lived in North America (and also in Central and South America)

About A.D. 982—Eric the Red, born in Norway, reaches Greenland during one of the first European voyages to North America

About 985—Eric the Red brings settlers from Iceland to Greenland

About 1000—Leif Ericson (Eric the Red's son) leads what is thought to be the first European expedition to mainland North America; Leif probably lands in Canada

1492—Christopher Columbus, sailing for Spain, reaches America

1497—John Cabot reaches Canada in the first English voyage to North America

1513—Ponce de León of Spain explores Florida

1519-1521—Hernando Cortés of Spain conquers Mexico

1565—St. Augustine, Florida, the first permanent European town in what is now the United States, is founded by the Spanish

1607—Jamestown, Virginia is founded, the first permanent English town in the present-day U.S.

1608—Frenchman Samuel de Champlain founds the village of Quebec, Canada

1609—Henry Hudson explores the eastern coast of present-day U.S. for The Netherlands; the Dutch then claim parts of New York, New Jersey, Delaware, and Connecticut and name the area New Netherland

1619—Virginia's House of Burgesses, America's first representative lawmaking body, is founded

1619—The first shipment of black slaves arrives in Jamestown

1620—English Pilgrims found Massachusetts' first permanent town at Plymouth

1621—Massachusetts Pilgrims and Indians hold the famous first Thanksgiving feast in colonial America

1622—Indians kill 347 settlers in Virginia

1623—Colonization of New Hampshire is begun by the English

1624—Colonization of present-day New York State is begun by the Dutch at Fort Orange (Albany)

1625—The Dutch start building New Amsterdam (now New York City)

1630—The town of Boston, Massachusetts is founded by the English Puritans

1633—Colonization of Connecticut is begun by the English

1634—Colonization of Maryland is begun by the English

1635—Boston Latin School, the colonies' first public school, is founded

1636—Harvard, the colonies' first college, is founded in Massachusetts

1636—Rhode Island colonization begins when Englishman Roger Williams founds Providence

1638—The colonies' first library is established at Harvard

1638—Delaware colonization begins when Swedish people build Fort Christina at present-day Wilmington

1640—Stephen Daye of Cambridge, Massachusetts prints *The Bay Psalm Book*, the first English-language book published in what is now the U.S.

1643—Swedish settlers begin colonizing Pennsylvania

1647—Massachusetts forms the first public school system in the colonies

1650—North Carolina is colonized by Virginia settlers in about this year

1650—Population of colonial U.S. is about 50,000

1660—New Jersey colonization is begun by the Dutch at present-day Jersey City

1670—South Carolina colonization is begun by the English near Charleston

1673—Jacques Marquette and Louis Jolliet explore the upper Mississippi River for France

1675-76—New England colonists beat Indians in King Philip's War

1682—Philadelphia, Pennsylvania is settled

1682—La Salle explores Mississippi River all the way to its mouth in Louisiana and claims the whole Mississippi Valley for France

1693—College of William and Mary is founded in Williamsburg, Virginia

1700—Colonial population is about 250,000

1704—*The Boston News-Letter*, the first successful newspaper in the colonies, is founded

1706—Benjamin Franklin is born in Boston

1732—George Washington, future first president of the United States, is born in Virginia

1733—English begin colonizing Georgia, their thirteenth colony in what is now the United States

1735—John Adams, future second president, is born in Massachusetts

1743—Thomas Jefferson, future third president, is born in Virginia

1750—Colonial population is about 1,200,000

1754—France and England begin fighting the French and Indian War over North American lands

1763—England, victorious in the war, gains Canada and most other French lands east of the Mississippi River

1764—British pass Sugar Act to gain tax money from the colonists

1765—British pass the Stamp Act, which the colonists despise; colonists then hold the Stamp Act Congress in New York City

1766—British repeal the Stamp Act

1770—British soldiers kill five Americans in the "Boston Massacre"

1773—Colonists dump British tea into Boston Harbor at the "Boston Tea Party"

1774—British close up port of Boston to punish the city for the tea party

1774—Delegates from all the colonies but Georgia meet in Philadelphia at the First Continental Congress

1775—**April 19:** Revolutionary war begins at Lexington and Concord, Massachusetts

May 10: Second Continental Congress convenes in Philadelphia

June 17: Colonists inflict heavy losses on British but lose Battle of Bunker Hill near Boston

July 3: George Washington takes command of Continental army

1776—**March 17:** Washington's troops force the British out of Boston in the first major American win of the war

May 4: Rhode Island is first colony to declare itself independent of Britain

July 4: Declaration of Independence is adopted

December 26: Washington's forces win Battle of Trenton (New Jersey)

1777—**January 3:** Americans win at Princeton, New Jersey

August 16: Americans win Battle of Bennington at New York-Vermont border

September 11: British win Battle of Brandywine Creek near Philadelphia

September 26: British capture Philadelphia

October 4: British win Battle of Germantown near Philadelphia

October 17: About 5,000 British troops surrender at Battle of Saratoga in New York

December 19: American army goes into winter quarters at Valley Forge, Pennsylvania, where more than 3,000 of them die by spring

1778—February 6: France joins the American side

July 4: American George Rogers Clark captures Kaskaskia, Illinois from the British

1779—February 23-25: George Rogers Clark captures Vincennes in Indiana

September 23: American John Paul Jones captures British ship *Serapis*

1780—May 12: British take Charleston, South Carolina

August 16: British badly defeat Americans at Camden, South Carolina

October 7: Americans defeat British at Kings Mountain, South Carolina

1781—January 17: Americans win battle at Cowpens, South Carolina

March 1: Articles of Confederation go into effect as laws of the United States

March 15: British suffer heavy losses at Battle of Guilford Courthouse in North Carolina; British then give up most of North Carolina

October 19: British army under Charles Cornwallis surrenders at Yorktown, Virginia as major revolutionary war fighting ends

1783—September 3: United States officially wins Revolution as the United States and Great Britain sign Treaty of Paris

November 25: Last British troops leave New York City

1787—On December 7, Delaware becomes the first state by approving the U.S. Constitution

1788—On June 21, New Hampshire becomes the ninth state when it approves the U.S. Constitution; with nine states having approved it, the Constitution goes into effect as the law of the United States

1789—On April 30, George Washington is inaugurated as first president of the United States

1790—On May 29, Rhode Island becomes the last of the original thirteen colonies to become a state

1791—U.S. Bill of Rights goes into effect on December 15

INDEX- *Page numbers in boldface type indicate illustrations.*

155

About the Author

Dennis Brindell Fradin is the author of more than 100 published children's books. His works for Childrens Press include the Young People's Stories of Our States series, the Disaster! series, and the Thirteen Colonies series. His other books are *Remarkable Children* (Little, Brown), which is about twenty children who made history, and a science-fiction novel entitled *How I Saved the World* (Dillon). Dennis is married to Judith Bloom Fradin, a high-school English teacher. They have two sons named Tony and Mike and a daughter named Diana Judith. Dennis was graduated from Northwestern University in 1967 with a B.A. in creative writing, and has lived in Evanston, Illinois, since that year.

Photo Credits

The Connecticut Historical Society, Hartford—66 (top)

Historical Pictures Service, Chicago—11 (top), 21, 25 (top), 34, 42, 43, 54, 60, 70, 77 (both photos), 86, 141

Historic St. Mary's City, Maryland—39, Jack Hevey; 47 (both photos), Dennis Caudill; 60, Janet Connor

Library of Congress—27 (bottom), 48, 81, 113, 116, 117

Maryland Department of Economic and Community Development—4 (both photos), 9 (both photos), 13 (both photos)

Maryland Historical Society, Baltimore—14, 31, 32, 73, 76, 111, 130, 143, 145, 146, 147, 148, 149

Maryland State Archives—37 (Md HRG 1558)

National Park Service—11 (bottom center, bottom)

The Newberry Library—66 (left)

North Wind Picture Archives—6, 7 (both photos), 8 (both photos), 11 (top center), 17, 18 (both photos), 19, 20, 22, 24, 25 (bottom right), 26, 27 (top), 30, 36, 38, 41, 45, 46, 49, 53, 55, 57, 59, 63 (both photos), 64, 67, 68, 72, 79, 80, 88, 89, 90, 91 (both photos), 94, 96, 97, 98, 99, 101 (both photos), 104, 107, 108, 109 (both photos), 112 (both photos), 115, 119, 121, 122, 126, 127, 128, 134, 136, 137 (both photos)

Photri—10

Virginia State Library and Archives—125

Horizon Graphics—maps on: 6, 22 (bottom left), 70 (bottom), 83

Cover art—Steven Dobson

Cover and Interior Design—Horizon Graphics